DATE DUE		
MAR 09 2012			

D1064115

James Madison

United States Presidents

James Madison

Mary Malone

Enslow Publishers, Inc.

44 Fadem Road   PO Box 38
Box 699   Aldershot
Springfield, NJ 07081   Hants GU12 6BP
USA   UK

Library of Congress Cataloging-in-Publication Data

Malone, Mary.
   James Madison / Mary Malone.
      p. cm. — (United States presidents)
   Includes bibliographical references and index.
   Summary: Chronicles the life and career of the fourth President with
emphasis on his many contributions to the government of the United States
including his role in writing the Constitution and the Bill of Rights.
   ISBN 0-89490-834-0
   1. Madison, James, 1751-1836—Juvenile literature. 2. Presidents—
United States—Biography—Juvenile literature. [1. Madison, James,
1751-1836.] I. Title. II. Series.
E342.M25 1997
973.5'1'092—dc21
[B]   96-39133
                                           CIP
                                           AC

Printed in the United States of America

10 9 8 7 6 5 4 3 2 1

Illustration Credits: Collection of the New-York Historical Society, p. 107;
Library of Congress, pp. 15, 24, 32, 43, 64, 87, 88, 96; National Archives,
pp. 10, 35; Smithsonian Institution, p. 59; University Archives, Swemm
Library, College of William and Mary, p. 30; Virginia Historical Society,
Richmond, Virginia, pp. 78, 110.

Source Document Credits: Crane Collection, Princeton University
Libraries, pp. 66, 76, 80, 93, 104, 112; Library of Congress, pp. 46, 95;
National Archives, p. 48.

Cover Illustration: White House Historical Association.

Contents

1

THE INAUGURATION

S hortly after daybreak on March 4, 1809, the people still asleep in Washington, D.C., were awakened by the boom of a cannon. That was the first salute of the day to the President-elect, James Madison. It was not likely, however, that the noise awakened him.

Madison was often wakeful at night. He would light a candle on his bedside table and read if he could not sleep. To him, the cannon shaking the city awake was a loud reminder that a new phase in his life was beginning. A small, quiet, soft-spoken man, Madison was different from the usual impression of a politician. He did not boast or swagger. His clothes were always black, from his buckled shoes to his high-crowned hat. Only his ruffled white shirt broke the dark sober look of a clergyman. But he was a statesman, although no great speaker like the famous Patrick Henry, nor a dashing figure like Alexander Hamilton. Mentally, however, James Madison was a giant. For thirty years, all of his public life, he had dealt with ideas, theories, reason, and logic. His remarkable feat in writing and explaining the United States Constitution in 1787 was what made him "the great little Madison."[1]

The task before him—four years of governing a still restless, sometimes unruly nation—was daunting. But James Madison was confident that whatever happened in the next few years would not break the ties of union among the states. That was the most important thing— the Union of the thirteen states that had survived the American Revolution and adoption of the Constitution.

Today he would be taking over the office that Thomas Jefferson was leaving. Like George Washington, Jefferson refused to consider a third term as President. Glad to return to his beloved house Monticello, Jefferson said he was happier on this day than Madison.[2] They were fellow Virginians, both of them plantation owners, and leaders of the Democratic-Republican party. Jefferson had chosen Madison to be his secretary of state. They worked together in harmony for eight years. Then Jefferson urged Madison to run for President. Madison did and was elected by a a large majority.

Of course, Madison knew well the dangers and problems of the presidency. He might not have chosen to be President, but he accepted it because he had always put the nation's welfare before his own. The Constitution, whose adoption had been a personal achievement for Madison twenty-two years before, was still being tested. As President he would, if necessary, uphold and protect it.

Fortunately, Madison's wife, Dolley, had no fear about the future. She had often served as President Jefferson's hostess in the President's House. Jefferson, a widower, kept social affairs at a minimum, but with Dolley Madison as First Lady, it would be very different now. She was looking forward to bringing back the receptions and dinner parties that Jefferson had avoided holding.

Well before noon on inauguration day, a troop of cavalry came to the Madisons' home on K Street to escort the presidential party to the Capitol. Hordes of people who had come to take part in the great day followed the Madison carriage on foot and on horseback. The streets were clogged with carriages and wagons. The Capitol building, still not completely finished, was jammed with government workers, politicians, foreign officials, and as many ordinary people as could be squeezed in.

Madison took the oath of office in a low tone that only those near him could hear. His wife looked beautiful and stylish in a white cambric dress and a purple bonnet. She was as calm and composed as ever as she listened to her husband's short speech. Madison's address to the crowd was described as "forcible but nervous."[3]

After the inauguration, James and Dolley Madison returned home. They held an open house all afternoon. Every room of their residence was filled with people who came for punch and cake as well as a word with the President. Outside, more people awaited their turn to go in.

There was not time for the President to rest before getting ready for the big gala, the inaugural ball that evening. Madison may have considered it a necessary evil, but Dolley Madison did not mind. She approved of

Madison took the oath of office on March 4, 1809, with his wife, Dolley, at his side.

celebrating her husband's inauguration. Held at Long's Hotel on the site of the present Library of Congress, this would be the first inaugural ball since George Washington's time.

Thomas Jefferson came early and was greeted by the band playing "Jefferson's March." The hotel was soon packed with people. When the Madisons arrived, the band struck up "Madison's March."

Dancing began, but there was scarcely room enough for it. The Madisons did not dance. They stood, bowing and shaking hands, greeting each person who could get close to them. Dolley Madison was radiant. She looked like a queen in her elegant, buff-colored velvet gown with a very long train, and a turban trimmed with plumes, said to have come from Paris. A pearl necklace, earrings, and bracelet completed her outfit. She stood between the President and seventeen-year-old Payne Todd. Payne was her son by her first marriage to John Todd.

As the festivities went on, Madison looked exhausted. A friend, Mrs. Margaret Bayard Smith, noticed how pale he was. She told him she wished she could offer him a seat. He said, so it is recorded, "I would much rather be in bed."[4] But then he quickly turned his remark into a joke, as he often did.

The evening wore on, and the air inside the hotel became stifling. Some people fainted. Attempts to open the windows failed, so the windowpanes were knocked out. The cool air rushing in revived the crowd. The

Madisons stayed for supper, but by midnight were ready to leave. Dolley Madison picked up her long train and she and the President led the way out. Thomas Jefferson had departed hours before. The party was over, although many guests stayed on.

The stormy presidency of James Madison had begun.

2

MADISON COUNTRY

Almost a hundred years before James Madison was born, his great-great-grandfather, James Maddison, left England for the Virginia Colony in the New World. He was granted many acres of land, something the Virginia Colony had plenty of, and was willing to give it away to worthy settlers. The first Maddison and his descendants, who dropped the second "d" in their name, added more land over the years. By 1751, when James Madison, Jr., was born, the Madison family owned five thousand acres of land in the fertile Piedmont section of Virginia and at least one hundred slaves.

James Madison, Sr., father of the future President, had inherited the plantation as had every oldest son in preceding generations. Besides being a planter, he was the leader of Orange County's militia, or nonprofessional army. He was a leading member of the established Church of England in his area. At home, he read the Bible to his children and escorted them to regular Sunday church services. He and his wife, Nelly Conway Madison, like most of the planter class, had many children. Fourteen were born to them; nine lived past infancy—five boys and four girls. The first child, James, Jr., always called "Jemmy" by his family, would be the one to inherit from his father. That was according to the law then observed in Virginia. As a child, Jemmy was rather sickly, subject to occasional seizures similar to epilepsy although not as serious. What he lacked in physical strength, however, Jemmy made up for in for intelligence. He was bright, curious about the animal and plant life on the plantation, and a great reader. He learned to read and write from his grandmother, Frances Taylor Madison, who lived with the family. Growing up, Jemmy had many playmates and companions: his own brothers and sisters as well as the slave children on the plantation. Jemmy and the two brothers nearest to him in age, Ambrose and Francis, met often with cousins who lived in nearby plantations or towns. They all learned to ride and handle horses— a necessity because horses provided the only means of land travel. Later, Jemmy learned to handle firearms. This was also a necessity in those days due to the danger of enemy raids on Virginia's western frontier during the French and Indian War (1754–1763).

As the family grew, Colonel Madison, as James, Sr., was called, had to build a bigger house on his estate. Called Montpelier (after a town in France), the new dwelling was situated on high ground. From the house, there was a magnificent view of the Blue Ridge Mountains, ten miles away. Later in life, James Madison claimed that the air of Montpelier was clearer and purer than anywhere else, more healthful than the humid Tidewater section on the Virginia coast.

Settled in their large, elegant new home, the Madisons entertained often, like most of the Virginia planter class. Large families meant there were relatives galore. Family gatherings could have as many as one hundred people present. Because they were separated

The Madisons' home was called Montpelier after a town in France.

by many miles (even twenty-five miles meant a day's travel on horseback) friends and relatives stayed overnight and often longer. Virginia hospitality included welcoming visitors for long visits and providing the best possible food and drink. Also part of Southern hospitality was keeping up with "connections," so important to Virginians of the upper class. These connections affected careers and politics, marriages and friendships.

In spite of the relative ease and comfort the plantation families enjoyed, and the fine climate of the Piedmont, there were some bad times too, especially the epidemics of smallpox, malaria, and yellow fever. "Ten times more terrible than Britons, Canadians, and Indians together," as John Adams, one of the nation's founders, said.[1] There was no real cure then for these diseases. In 1761, smallpox spread through Virginia. Luckily, Montpelier escaped the contagion at that time, but several Madison relatives died in the epidemic.

When Jemmy was eleven, Colonel Madison decided it was time for him to go away to school. "Plantation schools," which served the planters' children, were set up in different plantation homes throughout Orange County. Jemmy was sent to the Innes plantation, seventy miles from Montpelier. As the oldest child in his family, also the most studious, Jemmy would be provided with a good education. At the Innes school, he came to know Donald Robertson, the learned schoolmaster, who had graduated from Edinburgh

University in Scotland. Jemmy stayed at the school as a boarder for five years. Several other boys, including his five Taylor cousins, were there also. He learned a good deal from Mr. Robertson—not only advanced subjects like mathematics and science, but Latin, Greek, and French. Later he said of his first schoolmaster, "All I have been in life I owe largely to that man."[2]

3

THE BEST EDUCATION

W hen Jemmy arrived home from Mr. Robertson's school, he learned that his father had made plans for him. A young clergyman, Thomas Martin, had been engaged as a "family teacher" to instruct the younger children at home—and to prepare Jemmy for college.

Thomas Martin, only twenty-five years old himself, became a companion as well as a tutor for sixteen-year-old Jemmy. The two enjoyed discussing interesting topics of the day. Ever since the Stamp Act in 1765, which put a tax on all public documents, opposition to British rule had been growing in the colonies. Along with "taxation without representation," the colonists had to support a standing army of British soldiers.

After being tutored for two years, Jemmy was

considered qualified for college. Mr. Martin recommended the College of New Jersey, now Princeton University. He had graduated from that college, which had a reputation for being modern and progressive under its renowned president, Dr. John Witherspoon.

Colonel Madison liked what he heard about the college and decided that Jemmy should go there. In the summer of 1769, Jemmy; Thomas Martin and his brother Alexander Martin; and one of the Madison slaves, Sawney, left Montpelier for Princeton, New Jersey, three hundred miles away. They traveled on horseback, laden with luggage and Jemmy's books. The roads were bad, little more than trails. Several rivers had to be crossed by ferry. The group made overnight stays along the way. After they left Virginia, the travelers rode through Maryland, Delaware, eastern Pennsylvania, and New Jersey. By hard riding and long hours, they reached Princeton in ten days. The highlight of the trip for Jemmy was Philadelphia. He was impressed by the city's fine buildings, paved streets, and lights at night—its big-city air. With a population of forty thousand, it was said to be next to London in size.

Arriving finally at Nassau Hall in Princeton, Jemmy was assigned to a room that he would share with two other young men. After his traveling companions and Sawney left, he arranged, as suggested by Thomas Martin, to take an examination. If he passed, he could enter college as a sophomore rather than a freshman. His excellent education before coming to Princeton had prepared him well, and he passed the examination easily. Soon, he would begin classes. The curriculum included courses in science, written and oral expression, public discussion, living languages, the study of society, and the work of great writers. Although Jemmy's voice was not strong enough for public discussion, he excelled at writing arguments for his debating team. He adjusted well to his new environment and took part in the usual student activities. Soon, noting that prices in Princeton were higher than expected, he wrote home for more money. He was always mindful of addressing his father as "Honored Sir," and ending his letters as "Your Affectionate Son."[1]

Dr. John Witherspoon soon got to know James Madison and recognized his ability. The young Virginian was influenced by the ideas of the outspoken Scotsman who, like his first teacher, had graduated from Edinburgh University. Witherspoon had much to say about virtue and justice, freedom of religion, and politics—especially the tyranny of vested power, such as Britain's policy toward the colonies. Most of the Princeton faculty, like Witherspoon, were anti-British and pro-American. They supported the rising tide of rebellion in the colonies. Seven years later, John Witherspoon would be one of the signers of the Declaration of Independence.

Madison made some good friends at college—John Hancock, the poet Philip Freneau, and William Bradford of Philadelphia, who became a special friend and later the United States attorney general. Aaron Burr, a child prodigy who entered Princeton at age thirteen, graduated with Madison's class at age sixteen.

At the end of his first year, James Madison decided to challenge himself by combining his junior and senior years into one. One reason may have been that at nineteen he was older and more mature intellectually than his classmates. Along with another student, Joseph Ross, he was granted permission to undertake this cram course. Like his companion, young Madison managed to survive it, but only at the price of affecting his health. By studying day and night, with only a few hours' sleep each night, he was so weakened he could not appear for his commencement exercises in October 1771.

He did not go home at once, fearing that he could not stand the rigorous journey. He wrote to his father, asking for permission to stay on at Princeton for graduate work. This was allowed and he began another round of studies, with learning the Hebrew language as his goal. However, after six months, his father wrote asking him to return home. Thomas Martin had to leave and Colonel Madison wanted his oldest son to take over as tutor of the younger children. Up to this time, Jemmy had not decided on a professional career. Neither of the two most popular choices for college-educated young men—the clergy and the law—appealed to him.

Back home, Jemmy was in "feeble" health, as he recalled, and the sudden attacks "resembling epilepsy," which had plagued him as a child, returned.[2] There is no record of his having suffered such spells while he was at Princeton. One of his biographers believed that it was not epilepsy that Madison had, but a nervous disorder that could be triggered by trauma, such as over-study.[3] That, and missing the mental stimulation of Princeton, probably accounted for Madison's poor health and low spirits.

He kept up a correspondence with William Bradford, his friend from Princeton. He learned that Joe Ross, his companion in his advanced studying at college, had died. That news brought on a deepening depression. He wrote back to Bradford mentioning his health worries. He was "dull and infirm," he said, and did not expect to have a long life.[4] Bradford replied, trying to encourage him by saying that people with poor health often lived to an old age while healthier people died young.

Colonel Madison sent his ailing son to the warm springs of Bath in northern Virginia. The young man took the treatment and drank plenty of mineral water. He did feel somewhat better then, and his doctor told him to engage in more activity, less study. Madison followed that advice and began riding his horse around the plantation, spending hours outdoors. His health gradually improved, although it was never vigorous. But it did not occupy his mind to the exclusion of other important activities.

Madison never gave up his dedication to reading and study. History, especially the history of ancient and medieval governments—and how they rose and

James Madison was fascinated by the history of ancient and medieval governments.

fell—fascinated him. Exciting new ideas in the Age of Enlightenment dawning in Europe, especially France, were also of great interest to young James Madison. The principles of freedom, reason, democracy, and government by the people instead of kings all promised great changes in America in the not too distant future. He hoped to take part in bringing about such changes.

4

A CAREER IN POLITICS

S omething occurred in 1774 that did much to arouse young James Madison from his low spirits. Through his father's influence, he was appointed to a position on the Orange County Committee of Safety. He was assigned to travel around the county and check on the observance of the boycott of English goods. His brother, Ambrose, took James's place as Colonel Madison's assistant in running the plantation. That suited James, Jr., just fine.

Reading and study were put aside for a time as young Madison engaged in more active pursuits. He was becoming deeply concerned about the effects on the colonies of King George III's tyranny. The colonies' governors, appointed by the Crown, reflected the policies of the king. As he rode about Orange County,

Madison learned about the widespread discrimination against people who did not belong to the established Church of England. All the citizens of Virginia were taxed for the upkeep of that religion. Those who protested were often imprisoned. Madison remembered how religious freedom was often discussed—and supported—at Princeton. He believed it was unfair to discriminate against any religion, especially in a colony like Virginia where many people spoke about liberty and freedom.

The colonies as a whole were moving ever closer to war with England. In the Boston Massacre of 1770, American colonists demonstrating against the Crown's arrogant tax policy were shot down by British soldiers. The Boston Tea Party of 1774 was another act against the British policy of taxation without representation. At Boston Harbor, colonists dressed as Mohawks dumped overboard a cargo of tea from England. The tea would have been subject to the hated tax. The British authorities reacted by closing the port of Boston. The colonists then did not hesitate to send delegates to the first Continental Congress when it met in Philadelphia. They had an agenda.

James Madison admired the Massachusetts colonists' revolt and their contempt for the British government four thousand miles away.

Armed conflict began with the Battle of Lexington and Concord in 1775. Madison, at twenty-four, wanted to join the Virginia militia, but his health problems prevented that. He turned to public service in aid of the American cause. He knew he could and would, in spite of a weak body and a small voice, speak out for liberty. His opinions were already becoming known to the Orange County citizens he met daily. As a result, in May 1776, he was chosen as a delegate to attend a convention in Williamsburg called to adopt a new constitution for Virginia.

While in Williamsburg, Madison lived with his second cousin, the Reverend James Madison, president of the College of William and Mary.[1]

It was in May 1776 at the Williamsburg Convention that, as Madison said later, he entered public life and developed "a taste for politics that would never desert him."[2] He was twenty-five years old. The meeting was attended by the foremost citizens of Virginia—among them Edmund Pendleton, George Mason (who would become Madison's mentor), Patrick Henry, and Thomas Jefferson.

The movement for independence was strong in Virginia, and there was much talk about it at the convention. As one of the youngest members there, Madison was usually too shy to speak publicly. He did, however, stand up for Thomas Jefferson's proposal to declare religious freedom and an end to the established religion. That recommendation was put off by the convention. In later years, Madison said it was he who had suggested that the word "toleration," which was then proposed, be exchanged for "free exercise of religion."[3]

Madison lived in the President's House at the College of William and Mary while attending the Williamsburg Convention in 1776.

His suggestion was not fully acceptable until years later when he was elected to the Virginia House of Delegates. He then succeeded in passing Jefferson's bill for religious freedom and the end to tax-supported religion.

At Williamsburg young Madison listened closely most of the time, learning a great deal from his elders in the convention. He agreed with the proposal to instruct the Virginia delegates at the Continental Congress in Philadelphia to declare independence from

Britain. That bold action had a dramatic effect. The Congress quickly appointed a committee to write a declaration stating the independence of the colonies. Thomas Jefferson, who was then a member of the Continental Congress and noted for his skill with words, was drafted to write the document. Called the Declaration of Independence, it was released on July 4, 1776. It became the clarion call for the thirteen colonies to cut all ties to the British Crown and to strike out on their own.

After the Declaration of Independence was issued, the Continental Congress started work on a project that was more difficult—the Articles of Confederation for the new, independent United States of America. It took quite a long time before a document was ratified. Although imperfect, the Articles did keep the colonies— by that time states—together until the Constitution as we know it was written in 1787. The Articles of Confederation were in existence during the American Revolution, which lasted until 1783.

The war did not go well at first for the Americans. The much stronger British forces took New York and held on to it. They blockaded the coast. It was not until the Battle of Trenton in December 1776 that the American Army, under General George Washington, won an important victory. Washington, however, had to beg Congress for money, food, and supplies for his troops. Under the Articles of Confederation, the

George Washington was commander of the American Revolutionary Army and chairman of the Constitutional Convention.

Congress had no power to raise money or to enforce laws to levy (legally establish and collect) taxes.

At Williamsburg, the House of Delegates was established under the new Constitution for Virginia. As a participant in the original convention, Madison became a member of Virginia's new Assembly and served for one term. Then he had to run for election. A more experienced politician, wise to the ways of voters, had provided them with a keg of rum when they came to vote.[4] Madison had never considered such a thing, although it was a long-time custom, and he lost the election. His biographers believe that from then on, he observed the tradition. At any rate, he never lost another election.

However, Madison had made a favorable impression on the delegates at the Williamsburg Convention. His intelligence and reasoning, although not loudly proclaimed, were noted. He was appointed to the Virginia Council of State. As one of eight members of the Council, he gave advice and information to the governor, Patrick Henry, and then to Henry's successor, Thomas Jefferson. Madison learned early that he and Patrick Henry disagreed on many vital matters, especially states' rights versus national rights. That topic would arise often when a national constitution was being formed.

With Thomas Jefferson as Virginia's governor, the long friendship between Madison and Jefferson was established. Although they were unlike in many ways, their appearance was the most noticeable difference.

Jefferson was over six feet tall, and rugged; Madison no more than five feet six inches, and slight. Jefferson was impulsive and open; Madison was cautious, reserved, and slower to act. But the two shared political ideals. They were of the same privileged class, neighbors (only twenty-seven miles apart in the Piedmont area of Virginia), great readers and scholars, political radicals for their time and place, and children of the Age of Enlightenment.

The two years Madison served on the Council of State provided valuable experience for him which helped in overcoming some of his shyness and lack of public-speaking skill.

In 1779, James Madison left the Virginia legislature after he was elected as a delegate from Virginia to the Second Continental Congress. That was a big step forward in his career and gave him national prominence. At age twenty-eight, he was one of the youngest delegates. Moving to Philadelphia, where the Congress was held, marked the first time Madison had left Virginia since his college days.

He was now at the center of national events, part of the government that was directing the war. As the war continued, the movement to win France as an ally of the American cause finally succeeded in 1778. Benjamin Franklin had been appointed ambassador to France mainly for the purpose of obtaining official French support. With the help of the French army and navy the American forces drove the British from New York, broke the coastal blockade, and won battles in the South where the British forces had retreated. The fighting ended with the surrender of Lord Cornwallis at Yorktown in October 1781. The peace treaty was not signed until 1783.

While in the Continental Congress, Madison noted that the members could seldom agree or get together on

James Madison left the Virginia legislature in 1779 after he was elected as a delegate to the Second Continental Congress.

any policy. Many of the delegates voted for their own or their states' interests instead of for the nation's best interests. There were arguments over tariffs (schedules of tax rates for goods), the western boundaries of the states, the debts owed by individual states, and the permanent place for a national capital. Madison was kept busy with formal reports, writing to the state governments, and shaping diplomatic instructions, especially to the French ambassador. He was the one selected to translate the French communications into English.

While he was in Philadelphia, Madison lived in a boardinghouse, where several delegates to Congress stayed. Among the residents was the family of William Floyd, a delegate from New York State. One of Floyd's three daughters, sixteen-year-old Kitty, attracted the young men in the house, especially in the evenings when she played the harpsichord. Madison was smitten and soon began to court the young woman. She encouraged him to the point of accepting his proposal of marriage. Her father approved and the wedding date was set for November 1783. Madison wrote to Jefferson, back in his home Monticello by this time, telling him about the engagement. Jefferson congratulated his friend.

In the summer preceding the wedding, the Floyd family made a trip back to New York. When Madison received a letter from Kitty, he learned she had broken their engagement and had accepted the proposal of a young clergyman. The rejection was painful, but Madison revealed his disappointment only to Jefferson. His letter was answered by a consoling reply. Jefferson indicated that there would be other opportunities for happiness. In later years, not long before his death, Madison's secretary collected his letters. When that letter to Jefferson turned up, Madison crossed out the lines in it relating to his broken engagement.

Soon after, when his term expired in October 1783, Madison left the Continental Congress and returned to Virginia. For the first time in four years, he saw Montpelier again. He was welcomed by his family. He may have thought his career in public service was over. In fact, it had hardly begun. At home for a while, he buried himself in study and in books that had been sent to him from Paris by Jefferson, who had been appointed American ambassador to France. Madison read about the laws and governments of other times and places. Why, he asked himself, had governments set up to involve the people failed? Why had some succeeded at first, only to fail later? One of his biographers asked a question about Madison's concentrated study of governments. "Why did James Madison become a literary politician rather than a literary planter?" The answer to that was because "he was caught up in the swirl of a great political storm . . . brought to his life work without knowing exactly when the choice was made."[5]

5

THE
CONSTITUTION

A t Montpelier, Madison settled down to read and study during a cold winter that prevented much outdoor activity. He found himself pondering the nation's faltering government. The Articles of Confederation, which had served well enough during the American Revolution, were no longer working as a constitution for the new nation. Congress had no power to enforce laws, to raise money and pay its debts, to stabilize the currency, or to regulate commerce among the states. Each state carried on its own government, refused to pay necessary funds to Congress, and set up its own system of tariffs and taxes. There was no federal court, no Senate, and no President. Above all, Madison wondered whether the states could really work together in the Continental Congress. Could they secure the life, liberty, and pursuit of happiness promised in the Declaration of Independence if each state went its own way?

In the spring of 1784, the voters of Orange County urged Madison to stand for election to the Virginia House of Delegates. He agreed to run and won the election. One of his first actions was to propose that Virginia invite the other states to come to a meeting to discuss how to change or amend the Articles of Confederation. As the largest and most powerful state, Virginia carried a great deal of weight throughout the country, and would be heard.

Some in the House of Delegates opposed the idea, especially Patrick Henry, who was then the governor and a firm believer in states' rights. He feared giving too much power to a national government, and he knew that Madison believed only a strong national government could survive. Thomas Jefferson was now far away in Paris. He would support Madison, even if he might question having a too-powerful federal government. Jefferson had been urging Madison to come to Paris for a visit. However, the prospect of a two-month-long sea voyage and its effect on his uncertain health prevented Madison from accepting his friend's invitation. It seems likely, too, that Madison did not want to miss being present when constitutional action was likely to happen.

The House of Delegates approved Madison's proposal. Although only a few states sent representatives to the meeting in Annapolis, Maryland, an important mission was accomplished. As requested, Congress did call for a larger convention of all the states to reconsider the Articles of Confederation. Called the Constitutional Convention, it was to be held in Philadelphia in May 1787.

Earlier that year, a group of angry farmers in western Massachusetts, led by Daniel Shays, had marched on the state capital. Unable to pay their debts because the current paper money was almost worthless, they threatened open warfare. The state militia arrived in time to prevent large-scale bloodshed, but the event, known as Shays's Rebellion, had shaken the delegates who came to the Constitutional Convention. They were ready to listen to demands for change. All of the states except Rhode Island responded to the call for a convention.

James Madison was the first to arrive in Philadelphia, early in May 1787. He returned to the same boardinghouse where he had stayed before.

Dignified Edmund Randolph, who became Virginia's governor in 1786, was appointed spokesman for his state's delegates at the convention. He would introduce the resolution known as the Virginia Plan. George Washington, revered by the whole country for his role in winning the War for Independence, was elected president of the convention. His presence alone inspired confidence. Other well-known delegates were Alexander

Hamilton from New York and John Jay, who later became the first Chief Justice of the Supreme Court.

James Madison, although only thirty-six years old, was described as "experienced in state and national politics, learned in political history and theory, a student of the law, (although not a lawyer), owner of landed property."[1] It has been said that "no man went to the Convention better prepared than Madison."[2] He was also "one of the least wealthy of the delegates."[3] Unlike some of the others, Madison had no connection with business. He was not in debt, nor a speculator. He held no stock or interest-bearing loans that would produce any conflict of interest.

Most of the delegates were young men in their thirties and forties. The oldest of all was Benjamin Franklin who, at eighty-one, had a lifetime of service to his country behind him. He provided a balance to the young men's impatience. He was one of five delegates at the Constitutional Convention who had signed the Declaration of Independence. John Adams from Massachusetts was another.

It soon became apparent that many delegates, including Madison, preferred to draft an entirely new constitution instead of patching up the old one. Opposition to a new document gradually stopped, and the task of writing it began. It took over one hundred days in the humid heat of a Philadelphia summer. Madison, emerging from the retiring silence of his younger days, spoke two hundred times. He was always

At age eighty-one, Benjamin Franklin was the oldest delegate to the Constitutional Convention.

ready with logical reasons for his stand on the questions discussed. Forgetting his weak voice and insignificant appearance, he commanded attention. When he spoke, the others present moved closer to hear him. His arguments made sense, revealing his wide knowledge of governments, old and new.

The Virginia Plan, which based a state's representation on its population, was largely Madison's brainchild. In order to make the central government stronger, he proposed dividing it into three separate branches. The legislative branch, Congress, would make the laws. There would be two parts of the legislative branch—the Senate and the House of Representatives. The people would vote directly for members of both houses. The second branch would be the executive, headed by a President, and the third would be the judicial branch, to judge the laws.

The Virginia Plan was approved by the larger states: Virginia, New York, and Pennsylvania. The smaller states, led by William Paterson of New Jersey, objected. They feared the Virginia Plan would give the large states too much power in the legislative branch, based on their greater population. The small states preferred the New Jersey Plan, which gave equal representation to all the states—as had existed under the old Articles of Confederation.

Compromises had to be made. Madison never held out for his own ideas if a middle ground could be arranged and something rather than nothing could pass. Each side had to win something. Roger Sherman of Connecticut proposed the compromise that was finally accepted. The Senate would have equal representation from every state; the House of Representatives would be based on each state's population.

Other compromises would be made. The executive branch would be represented by a President, not a king. There would be limited terms for the President and the legislative branch, and frequent elections. The powers of each branch of government—executive, judicial and legislative—were spelled out. There would be a balance of power among them, with no one branch able to control without challenge from the others.

There had to be a compromise about continuing the slave trade. The abolitionists of New England and other people in the North wanted it stopped at once. Even some prominent Virginians, like George Mason and James Madison, favored that plan. Both slaveholders themselves, they would welcome ending slavery by abolishing the selling of slaves. Mason said it was "dishonorable"[4] to the American character and Madison agreed, declaring that the federal government should have the power to prevent the increase of slavery.[5]

The Southern, slave-holding states protested that viewpoint and threatened secession, breaking away from the other states, if it came to pass. Their economy depended on slave labor. The compromise accepted by

SOURCE DOCUMENT

Saturday July 14. contin.?

from the Eastern States to the Western Country. and did not wish those remaining behind to be at the mercy of these Emigrants. Besides foreigners are resorting to that Country, and it is uncertain what turn things may take there. — On the question for agreeing to the motion of Mr. Gerry. it passed in the negative.

Mass. ay. Con. ay. N. J. no. Pa. divd. Del. ay. Md ay. Va. no. N. Ca. no. S. C. no. Geo. no.

Mr. Rutledge proposed to reconsider the two propositions touching the originating of money bills, & the equality of votes in the 2cond. branch.

Mr. Sherman was for the question on the whole at once. It was he said a conciliatory plan, it had been considered in all its parts, a great deal of time had been spent on it, and if any part should now be altered, it would be necessary to go over the whole ground again.

Mr. L. Martin urged the question on the whole. He did not like many parts of it. He did not like having two branches, nor the inequality of votes on the 1st branch. He willing however to make trial of the plan, rather than do nothing.

Mr. Wilson traced the progress of the report through its several stages, remarking yt. on the question concerning an equality of votes, the House was divided. our constituents had they voted as their representatives did, would have stood as 2/3 agst. the equality, and 1/3 only in favor of it. This fact would one day be known, and will it appear that this fundamental point has been carried by 1/3 agst. 2/3. What hopes will our constituents entertain when they find that the essential principles of justice have been violated in the outset of the Governmt. As to the privilege of originating money bills, it was not considered by any as of much moment, and by many as improper in itself. He hoped both clauses wd. be reconsidered. The equality of votes was a point of such critical importance, that every opportunity ought to be allowed, for discussing and collecting the mind of the Convention on it.

Mr. L. Martin denies that there were 2/3 agst. the equality of votes. The States that pleased to call themselves large, are the weakest in the Union. Look at Massts. Look at Virga. "are they efficient States?" He was for letting a separation take place if they desired it. He had rather there should be two confederacies, than one founded on any other principle than an equal 5

Madison in order to save the Union from falling apart was to stop the slave trade, but not before 1808.

No publicity was allowed to leak out from the convention hall. Keeping the whole process secret, Madison explained, allowed members to change their minds from one day to another without blame or criticism from the public or the newspapers.

For one hundred days, Madison held to a rigorous schedule. Besides his frequent speaking and writing, he took his own notes, not depending on the secretary, William Jackson. He wrote down every aspect of the events at the convention and the highlights of every speech. In the evenings he rewrote his notes, clarifying and smoothing the language. Then there were more meetings almost every night, with groups or individuals. "It almost killed me," Madison said later, but he was satisfied with the outcome.[6] Most of his proposals, first outlined in the Virginia Plan, prevailed in the first version of the Constitution.

On September 17, 1787, all the delegates present (three were absent) signed the document, which was read and reread, polished in style, and made ready for announcement to the public. Of course, criticism came from the public, especially the antinationalists, still strong in their states' rights position.

To explain the Constitution to the people and to persuade them that ratification was necessary, three men who had been prominent at the Convention took on a

SOURCE DOCUMENT

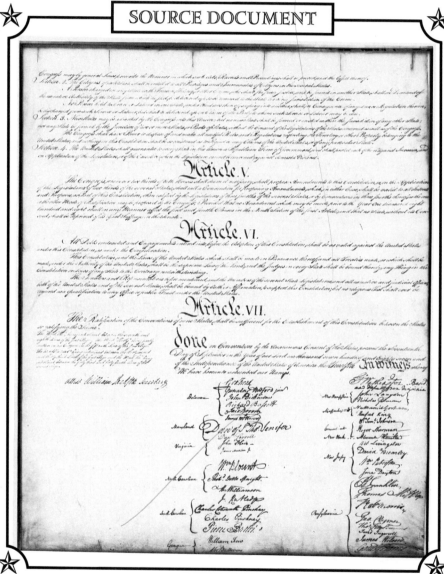

The last page of the United States Constitution shows signatures of the states' representatives.

big job. Alexander Hamilton, James Madison, and John Jay wrote a series of articles for the newspapers. Later, their articles were collected in a book called *The Federalist Papers*. This book has been called the clearest explanation of the Constitution, and one of the most important books published in the United States.

In his essays (he wrote twenty-nine out of eighty-five) Madison emphasized the advantages of a strong Union and explained the powers and structure of the federal government. He said that such a representative government would preserve freedom in a nation larger than the present one as well as it would preserve freedom in the United States as it was that year, in 1787. (This was an important point, as people expected the United States to grow.) Under this new form of government, no one interest (out of many) would be able to control the central government. The diversity of different factions would prevent tyranny.

The new Constitution had to be ratified or formally approved, by nine of the thirteen states before becoming law. Ironically, Virginia hesitated to ratify. When Madison learned that Patrick Henry was opposing ratification, he hurriedly left for Virginia and spoke in the House of Delegates with enough logic and reason to defeat the opposition. A strong Union, he said, upheld by the Constitution, did not cancel states' rights. The compromises made at the Constitutional Convention were enacted to balance the powers of each. On June 25, 1788, Virginia ratified the Constitution, believing it was the pivotal ninth state to save the Constitution. Later, it was learned that New Hampshire had ratified on June 21, 1788.

The Constitutional Convention had accomplished its purpose: the adoption of a Constitution for a government of the people. This was a new idea in the eighteenth century. "When compared with [other] forms of government that existed in the rest of the world . . . in a day when nearly every other government held to the principle of monarchy [with its] belief in the divine right of kings,"[7] the American Constitution was indeed a radical departure from tradition.

In January 1789, elections were held for President. George Washington was the overwhelming choice of the people. He received many more votes than John Adams, the runner-up, who was then named Vice President. The clause in the Constitution permitting this was amended later, when political parties emerged with differing policies and sometimes opposite viewpoints.

In February 1789, the members of Congress were elected. Madison wanted to be part of the new government and he was nominated for one of the two positions of United States senator from Virginia. However, also according to the Constitution, each state legislature (in Virginia called the House of Delegates) voted for its senators. Patrick Henry, although no longer governor of Virginia, had great influence in the legislature, enough to destroy Madison's candidacy. Madison then ran for election (by the people) as a

Virginia congressman in the House of Representatives. To defeat him, Patrick Henry pushed James Monroe into the race, in order to divide the votes against Madison. Fortunately that did not happen and Madison won anyway.

George Washington's inauguration took place in Federal Hall in New York City, then the temporary capital of the country, on April 10, 1789. James Madison, as one of the representatives from Congress, was in the procession following Washington. He had had a great deal to do with the event. He had impressed Washington at the Constitutional Convention with his knowledge and sound judgment as well as his skill in the use of language. Some time before the inauguration, Washington had sent for him, inviting him to stay at Mount Vernon and help with the inaugural address. Madison decided that the speech Washington had written was too long and recommended discarding it. He himself wrote a shorter, dignified speech that Washington liked, and later delivered at the inaugural ceremony.

Washington asked for Madison's advice on several other matters too, especially on making and writing speeches. When Washington delivered an address at the opening of Congress, his advisor Madison again wrote the speech. Then Madison composed the reply Congress sent to the President, and also the President's acknowledgment of it.

"Starting the new government from scratch" was a

difficult task for the first Congress.[8] The nation was nearly bankrupt. War loans from foreign governments were due. After much debate, the first tariff bill was passed, with Madison's help, and the government finally had an income. He then succeeded in having legislation passed to create the state, treasury, and war departments, and the federal court system. He also won on the question of the permanent location of the capital. It would be on the Potomac River where Madison (and the other Virginians) wanted it to be, not in New York or Philadelphia, the temporary location. The new capital city, to be called Washington, would be built on land given to the government by Virginia and Maryland.

Madison became a leader in the House of Representatives through his knowledge, his willingness to compromise, and his focus on the need for immediate action. A New England representative wrote that James Madison was "a thorough master of almost every public question that can arise, or he will spare no pains to become so, if he happens to be in want of information."[9]

Of all his accomplishments in helping to set the first Congress on a steady course, the Bill of Rights was his greatest achievement. During the hectic last days of the Constitutional Convention, some legislators, notably George Mason of Virginia, proposed adding a list of human rights to the Constitution. Madison was anxious to get the document ratified quickly and promised he would work for the addition of such rights to the

Constitution after it was ratified. He later kept his word, but he faced a difficult task. "We are in a wilderness without a single footstep to guide us," he wrote to his father.[10]

After collecting two hundred proposed additions of civil rights to the Constitution, Madison condensed them to ten amendments that covered guarantees for personal liberties. In December 1791, they were ratified, signed by the President, and added to the Constitution. The most important rights were contained in the first amendment—items such as freedom of religion, speech, and the press as well as the rights to assemble and to petition for redress of grievances. The tenth amendment stated that all powers not delegated to the United States are returned to the states or the people.

Freedom of religion, as guaranteed in the first amendment, was an issue especially important to Madison. From the beginning of his career, he had advocated it and opposed an established church. The issue of separation of church and state, however, is still with us in the 1990s, and its relevance to the Constitution is still debated.

Before the Bill of Rights ratification, in May 1791, Congressman Madison and his friend Thomas Jefferson, now secretary of state, took a vacation together. Madison had proposed it, and Jefferson readily agreed. They would tour the northeastern region of the country, going as far as the Canadian border.

Both men needed a rest from government matters, for the sake of their "health, recreation, and curiosity."[11] Leaving New York City, they sailed up the Hudson River to Poughkeepsie, where they met Jefferson's servant (slave) James Hemings, who had gone ahead on land, driving their loaded carriage. Then the three continued north by horseback, carriage, and often by water on sloops and ferries. They stayed overnight at comfortable inns. After reaching Vermont and facing head winds on Lake Champlain, they returned by an alternate route.

All along, they visited farms, factories, and homes. They kept journals, asked many questions, were welcomed by prominent officials, and recognized as the famous Americans they were. They even went fishing a few times. In just over a month, Madison and Jefferson traveled nine hundred miles on a vacation long remembered.

6

HOME
AND FAMILY

I n 1794, James Madison met and married Dolley Payne Todd. She was a twenty-six-year-old widow with a three-year-old son named Payne Todd. Her husband John Todd and a newborn son had died in a terrible yellow fever epidemic that swept through Philadelphia in the summer of 1793. Dolley and young Payne survived the epidemic, and in time Dolley's natural beauty and cheerful manner returned. She became the guardian for her thirteen-year-old sister Anna. Their father, John Payne, had died after moving his family from Virginia to Philadelphia, and Mrs. Payne had to take in boarders to support several children.

Dolley Todd's good looks attracted many admirers. She had dark hair clustered in ringlets around her face, a pink and white complexion, and deep blue eyes. She was tall, with a full figure. Her best friend, Elizabeth Collins, declared that when Dolley went out, "Gentlemen would station themselves where they could see her pass."[1] Dolley was not concerned by the stares she attracted, but one day she was somewhat perturbed by a note from a friend, Aaron Burr. He had lived in her mother's boardinghouse when he was a senator from New York State. Now he was requesting her permission for a visit that very evening from him and his friend, James Madison, who wanted to meet her. Dolley accepted the request, then sent word to her friend, Elizabeth, imploring her to be present that evening when Burr and Madison arrived. Elizabeth Collins came, and described Dolley as looking lovely in a dark mulberry-colored gown that set off her rosy complexion and sparkling eyes.

By the end of the evening, Madison was sure he wanted to marry Dolley Todd, and she was sure he would ask her. When he did, not long afterward, she was still uncertain, and took four months to make up her mind. Rumors of the possible engagement spread through Philadelphia, and Dolley received an invitation to tea from Lady Washington, as President George Washington's wife Martha was known. She urged Dolley to accept Madison's proposal. In spite of the seventeen-year difference in age he would make her a good husband, Lady Washington said.

Dolley Todd and James Madison were married on September 15, 1794, at the Virginia home of her sister,

Lucy, who had married George Washington's nephew. Writing to her friend Elizabeth that evening, Dolley said,

> In the course of this day, I gave my hand to the man who of all others I most admire . . . In this union, I have everything that is soothing and grateful in prospect— and my little Payne will have a generous and tender protector.[2]

After their marriage, the Madisons traveled back to Philadelphia. James Madison was still in Congress. In that era, the journey took three days from Virginia over roads so rough that Madison's new carriage was damaged.

Their first house was a rented one belonging to James Monroe, who at that time was ambassador to France. He had succeeded Thomas Jefferson after Jefferson had become President Washington's secretary of state. Soon the Madisons moved to a large, fashionable house on Spruce Street. They furnished it in the latest French style, with furniture Monroe sent them from Paris. Besides little Payne and Anna Payne, the family often included Madison's youngest sister Fanny, who stayed with them for long periods.

Dolley began to entertain in her new house and became known for her afternoon teas and her dinner parties. Everyone who knew her praised her friendliness. It was noted that her manner was a contrast to her husband's. He was serious and aloof except when he was with people he knew well. Then he became talkative and witty. He often told humorous stories about his political adventures. Although the Madisons might be called perfect opposites in personality, their marriage was a very happy one. Madison was proud of his wife's popularity and she was proud of his brilliant reputation in political affairs. He never protested about the money needed for lavish entertaining or the expense of Dolley's clothes. As a former Quaker (she had been expelled from the Society of Friends after her marriage to Madison, an "outsider"), Dolley Madison seemed to revel in the finery she had never had before. Now she often sent to Paris for her gowns and turbans and all the pretty decorations that were in fashion.

Madison also accepted the responsibility of young Payne Todd, and when the time came, sent him to a highly rated boarding school in Baltimore.

Madison's brother Ambrose had died suddenly in 1793, and their father was becoming more infirm. It was time now for James Madison, Jr., to attend to the management of the plantation. He saw that the mansion itself would have to be enlarged. He drew up plans, aided by Jefferson, who had designed and built his own home, Monticello. Wings were added to each side of Montpelier, and the house completely restored and refurnished. The elder Madisons and Fanny lived in the south wing, James and Dolley Madison in the north wing. It was a friendly and happy relationship.

Back in Philadelphia, which had become the capital of the government after New York and remained the

Dolley Madison was known for her beautiful formal gowns. This one is now on display in the Smithsonian Institute.

capital until 1800, George Washington was completing his second term, which he had reluctantly accepted in 1792. In 1796, John Adams was elected President and Washington retired to Mount Vernon. A rift had developed between Washington and James Madison. John Adams (the Vice President) and Alexander Hamilton (the secretary of the treasury) had converted Washington to their Federalist views favoring a national bank and a strong military.

Madison criticized Hamilton's reaction to a short uprising known as the Whiskey Rebellion. In 1794, some farmers in Pennsylvania protested the high tax imposed on the whiskey they made by distilling their surplus corn. They refused to pay the tax and threatened to use force, but were quickly put down by federal forces called out by Washington and Hamilton. Although Madison had no sympathy for the so-called rebellion, he called the event "a tempest in a teapot."[3] He feared Hamilton's talk about building a standing army might be enforced. That, Madison declared, would give too much power to the executive branch of government—and was unconstitutional besides.

Another source of contention between the two emerging parties—the Federalists and the Democratic-Republicans—was how to react to the British-French wars in Europe. Madison and his party were pro-French, especially because of the help from France during the American Revolution. Washington and Hamilton were pro-British. Madison felt that Britain was high-handed and arrogant—stopping American vessels on the high seas to search for deserters from the British navy, but often impressing (or kidnapping as indignant Americans said) American seamen.

The American shipping industry had expanded so greatly after the Revolution that the United States became a rival to Britain. Many British sailors deserted their navy for American ships. With the excuse of searching for those who had deserted, the Royal navy began stopping any American ship they encountered and dragging off deserters. Often, American seamen were taken off by force at the same time, "impressed" into service on British ships. If the Americans refused to allow the British to board, they faced the danger of being fired upon.

Chief Justice John Jay had been sent to London by Washington in 1794 to try to persuade Britain to stop such practices. The treaty he came back with (the Jay Treaty) was not popular. Madison opposed it. It was pro-British and anti-French, he said. It did not address the rights of neutral countries to be free of harassment by the British on the high seas. The claims about impressing American sailors were ignored. However, President Washington and the United States Senate signed the treaty. Jefferson was not around then to stand with Madison. He had resigned his post as secretary of state in 1793 after breaking with President Washington and the Federalist policies of John Adams and Alexander Hamilton.

His influence in Congress waning, Madison was "tired and discouraged."[4] When John Adams became President in 1796 after Washington's second term was over, Madison decided it was a good time for him to leave Congress. (Thomas Jefferson, who had been nominated for President as the candidate of the Democratic-Republicans, came in second to Adams and was, according to the system then, named as Vice President.) Completing his term in early 1797, Madison decided to leave Philadelphia and return to Virginia. When his retirement from Congress became known, his supporters in the Virginia Assembly assured him he could be unanimously elected governor of Virginia. He refused to consider that, or his certain election to the Virginia Assembly.

James Madison was now looking forward to a more relaxed even though busy life. His main interests would be centered on his family, his home, Montpelier, his crops, and making enough money to support his expensive lifestyle. He was ready now to take up his role as a Virginia planter. Soon he would be referred to as the "Squire of Montpelier," and Dolley, his wife, would become hostess of Montpelier. In time, she would be credited with making the place "one of the great centers of Virginia hospitality."[5]

7

SECRETARY OF STATE

If James Madison thought he had retired from government, he learned otherwise in 1800 when President John Adams lost his bid for a second term and Thomas Jefferson became President.

The election that year had resulted in a tie. Jefferson's rival was Aaron Burr, who had support from both Federalists and Democratic-Republicans. According to the new Constitution, the tie had to be broken by a vote in the House of Representatives. There was considerable support for Burr in the Congress. However, Alexander Hamilton, "who disliked Jefferson but knew Burr to be a rogue," influenced Congress to vote for Jefferson.[1] The result—Jefferson's election—made Alexander Hamilton the sworn enemy of Burr.

Immediately after becoming President, Jefferson

President Thomas Jefferson (pictured here) appointed James Madison to be secretary of state in 1800.

asked James Madison to be his secretary of state. How could Madison refuse to serve his best friend? Jefferson once said that he had no secrets from Madison. Madison agreed to Jefferson's request. With Thomas Jefferson as President and James Madison as secretary of state, the principles on which the Republic had been founded would be upheld.

However, Madison's new position meant leaving Montpelier and living for at least the next four years in Washington, D.C. Now the permanent home of the government, Washington was slowly rising from the low-lying marshland on the banks of the Potomac River.

Health problems again kept Madison inactive at home until after Jefferson's inauguration. Then, in February 1801, Colonel Madison died. As executor of his father's will, Madison, no longer "Jr.," had to settle the estate. The extensive land holdings were divided among his brother William, his sisters, and the surviving heirs of his deceased brothers, Ambrose and Francis. Madison's mother was well provided for and would continue to live in the south wing of the mansion. Nelly Conway Madison lived for twenty-eight years after her husband's death. James Madison kept Montpelier, the one hundred slaves who lived on the property, and five hundred acres of surrounding land.

When James and Dolley Madison finally left Montpelier in May 1801, they could not know that Washington would be their home for the next sixteen years. For some months, until a new house on F Street

Whenever James Madison wrote to Jefferson, he always addressed him as "Dear Sir."

was finished, the Madisons stayed in the President's House, by Jefferson's invitation.

Washington, D.C., was only partially built, still "almost a wilderness,"[2] and what was to become Pennsylvania Avenue was "a forest path."[3] Although Abigail Adams, President John Adams's wife, had called the new President's House "cold and uncomfortable,"[4] Jefferson had moved in and said it was a pleasant country residence, "free from the noise, the heat, the stench, and the bustle of a close-built town."[5] As a widower, Jefferson lived in spartan simplicity and did very little entertaining. He disliked formal affairs and dressed casually. He was described as wearing old worn carpet slippers when important callers arrived.

After a few months the Madisons settled in their new home, two blocks away from the President's House. Theirs was a comfortable three-story brick dwelling, with coach houses and stables in the rear, wine and coal rooms in the cellar, and space enough for Dolley's entertaining.

During President Jefferson's first term, the problem of conflict with Tripoli (now Libya) came up and was dealt with promptly. Prior to United States action, the Barbary Coast pirates of the North African Barbary States (Tripoli, Algiers, Morocco, and Tunis) demanded payment from merchant vessels entering Mediterranean waters. When the United States refused to go along with the routine tribute, Tripoli declared war and captured the American frigate, *Philadelphia*. President Jefferson and his secretary of state sent a naval force to bombard Tripoli. The leader, daring young Lieutenant Stephen Decatur, entered Tripoli Harbor and burned the captured ship. An overland campaign by the Americans completed the war against the Barbary pirates and ended the annual payment of tribute.

The problem of French and British harassment of American shipping was continuing and getting more serious. France and Britain each wanted to prevent American trade with the other country. They ignored American rights and treaties. Madison and Jefferson considered the British to be the worse offender, in attempting to blockade the American coast and to hold up American vessels at sea. With a navy that dominated the seas, Britain's actions seemed to claim the right to rule the shipping trade of its former colonies.

Protests from the United States only made the British more oppressive, announcing their Orders in Council, which stated that no neutral ship could trade with any country in Europe before stopping first in England for a license. The French responded to this by declaring they would seize any American ships that obeyed the Orders in Council. They also issued decrees to prevent American ships from entering French ports.

Jefferson and Madison felt that the United States was not yet strong enough to declare war on England. Instead, they succeeded in passing the Embargo Act, which kept American ships at home and out of danger. All commerce was stopped with England and France and even other neutral countries. The intention of the

Embargo Act was to hurt the two offending nations. Instead, it ruined the American economy. The New England states, which depended on free trade and the active exchange of exports and imports, were especially hurt.

This unhappy situation continued during Jefferson's presidency. United States ships were anchored all along the coast. The Federalists were furious. There were threats of secession, and many shippers disobeyed the law or engaged in smuggling.

One of the most important domestic accomplishments while Madison was secretary of state was Jefferson's purchase of the Louisiana Territory. Claimed by France, this tract of land (828,000 square miles) stretched from the Gulf of Mexico to the Rocky Mountains. Skillful diplomacy by the American representatives in Paris, Robert Livingston and James Monroe, brought about Napoleon's sale of the Louisiana Territory to the United States for the bargain price of $15 million. This marked the beginning of the American westward expansion to the Pacific. It was a "truly noble acquisition," Madison said.[6] Acquiring the Louisiana Territory was very popular with the American people, in spite of some criticism from the Federalists of New England. They feared that opening the vast lands to the west would favor the South and West more than the northeastern states. The Lewis and Clark expedition of 1804–1806 that explored the West and the far Northwest was another timely exploit. That gave the

United States a claim by right of exploration to the region beyond the Rocky Mountains. Then, in 1805, Jefferson sent Zebulon Pike to explore the Southwest, hopeful of expanding American authority there.

Although Jefferson, along with Madison, considered Florida to be part of the Louisiana Purchase, Spain still claimed it. Many Americans had already settled in Florida and wanted to be part of the Union. However, the President and his secretary of state would not take over Florida by force. They tried negotiating with Spain, but that country, with its internal problems, could not attend to the American requests. Acquisition of Florida by legal means was still many years ahead.

In 1804, a tragic occurrence shocked the nation. Alexander Hamilton was shot and killed in a duel with Aaron Burr. Unlike Hamilton, Burr did not hold his fire: he shot at close range the man who he believed had denied him the presidency in 1800. The public reaction was ruinous to Burr. Even though he defiantly kept his position as Vice President to Jefferson, his political career was over. At the end of Jefferson's first term, Burr departed for the West. Later, he was tried for treason after he attempted to set up a separate nation in the Mississippi Valley. Although he was acquitted for lack of evidence, he fled the United States and lived in exile in Europe for several years. He later returned to the United States.

All the problems that affected President Jefferson, Secretary of State Madison also endured. He was tired, overworked, and often in conflict with a fellow Virginian, John Randolph. Although he belonged to the same party as Madison, Randolph called himself an "Old Republican."[7] He opposed most of the Jefferson-Madison agenda. He called Madison a "visionary,"[8] and tried to discredit him by false accusations and rumors. One biographer described Randolph as "envious of [Madison's] . . . success."[9] Madison, with more important problems than an angry congressman, merely called Randolph "eccentric."[10]

Madison, like Jefferson, could not endure the hot, humid summers of Washington, D.C. Both of them took off for Virginia and their beloved Piedmont country as soon as summer began. Usually, Madison stayed at Montpelier until October. He felt that it was necessary for the benefit of his health to spend that time in the cooler, purer mountain air of his home.

At Montpelier, Dolley Madison was again in her element as hostess to all the relatives and friends who visited. She had had plenty of practice in Washington, acting as hostess for President Jefferson on many occasions as well as entertaining in her own home.

When Jefferson's second term drew to a close, he proposed James Madison as his successor. His influence convinced Madison that their party's continuance depended on the Madison-Jefferson "enlightenment"— with its belief in democracy and guarding the people's natural rights by a constitutional government of checks and balances.

8

PRESIDENT— FIRST TERM

Thomas Jefferson and James Madison, both devoted Democratic-Republicans who had actually founded the party, shared the same hopes for the nation. Although they did not always agree on the ways to bring about change, they usually arrived at the same conclusion. In the course of their association, Madison would point out to his idealistic friend the need for reality in politics as well as ideals. As Albert Gallatin, who would serve Madison as the strongest of his cabinet members, said, Madison was "slow in taking his ground, but firm when the storm rises."[1]

The Embargo Act, which was the source of much opposition in the country, continued in force until the last days of Jefferson's term. The Federalists were almost united in opposition to it and demanded repeal, or removal of the law. Madison did not agree. He felt war was the only alternative to embargo. Couldn't Americans endure whatever hardships the act imposed on them? However, in Congress the Federalists and their supporters, including John Randolph of Virginia, succeeded in repealing the Embargo Act. This would reopen the exchange of imports and exports with England and France. As these countries were still stopping American ships, repeal of the Embargo Act seemed like surrendering to wrongdoing.

Then, trying to defeat Madison for President, John Randolph convinced James Monroe to run for election as well. A rumor started that Madison would not make peace with England because he was secretly taking bribes from Napoleon. Madison made public his letters to James Monroe during the course of negotiations with England. They proved the accusation against him was groundless. Public opinion swung back to favor Madison. He was praised in several newspapers for his morals, dignity, moderation, and republican principles.[2] Monroe withdrew his name from the presidential race, and Madison was elected. He was inaugurated as the fourth President on March 4, 1809. He inherited all the problems Jefferson was glad to leave.

When Jefferson left office, he said, "Never did a prisoner released from his chains feel such relief as I shall in shaking off the shackles of power."[3] No wonder Madison looked gloomy on his inauguration day.

Foreign affairs would continue to be worrisome. After the unpopular Embargo Act forbidding American trade with the warring nations was repealed, the United States Congress substituted a Nonintercourse Act that empowered the President to restore trade with either country if it would stop harassing American commerce. Each country offered to stop its offenses against American shipping if the United States declared war on the other. Madison refused such an offer. He did not want war, but many people in the United States did. Some favored war with Britain, some with France, while still others wanted war declared on both nations. Madison kept trying, hoping for some compromise. Instead of declaring war, he repeated his conditions— lifting the ban on commerce with any nation that stopped seizing American ships and impressing American seamen on the high seas. France finally agreed to lift its decrees about seizing American ships that ventured into French ports and released the ships it had captured. England refused to release the sixty-two hundred American seamen being held. It seemed clear to Americans that the former "mother country" was determined to teach its former colonies a lesson by forcing them to obey unfair demands.

The times were certainly critical for the President. A declaration of war seemed to be the only response to

James Madison

SOURCE DOCUMENT

To Mrs Madison.   Washington August 17th 1809

My dearest,

We reached the end of our journey yesterday at one o'clock; without interruption of any sort on the road. Mr. Bolt had been here some time, one, if not two of the expected despatch vessels of England, had just arrived, and Mr. Gilston after a short passage from France, entered Washington about the moment I did. You may guess therefore the volumes of paper before us. I am but just dipping into them; and have seen no one as yet except Mr. Smith for a few minutes last evening. What number of days I may be detained here it is impossible to say. The period you may be sure will be shortened as much as possible. Every thing around and within reminds me that you are absent, and makes me anxious to quit the solitude. In my next I hope I shall be able to say when I shall have this gratification; perhaps also to say something of the intelligence just brought us. I send the paper of this morning which has something on the subject. I hope the communications of Gilston will be found more favorable than is stated. Those from England can scarcely be favorable, when such men hold the reins as we have lately had to do with. Mr and Mrs Erskine are still ? His successor had not sailed on the 20th of June.

God bless you and be assured of my constant affection

J Madison

James and Dolley wrote to each other whenever they were apart. Above is a letter to Dolley from James Madison written in 1809.

England's oppression. But Madison wanted desperately to avoid war.

He did his best to carry on the usual presidential activities, the social events the public expected and that Dolley Madison herself was eager to restore. The President's House was decorated, new furniture purchased, life-size portraits of the former Presidents installed. The Madisons entertained in style. They held weekly drawing-room receptions with buffets loaded with punch, cookies, ice cream, and fruit. Dinner parties were held often. Even with all of his problems, foreign and domestic, Madison often stood with his wife in the reception line. He never limited her entertaining, although his salary of $25,000 a year barely covered their expenses.

Dolley Madison was the hostess Washington loved. She was noted not only for her parties, but also for herself, her elegant gowns, and her fantastic turbans. Her manners were perfect. She was unfailingly gracious. She made the President's House the centerpiece of Washington society. Friends and associates were welcome at all times, even strangers if they carried a letter of introduction.

In spite of his ongoing foreign problems, President Madison and his family returned to Montpelier every summer. From July to October, the hottest months in Washington, he was able to restore his health and spirits. He also could visit Jefferson at Monticello, and the two talked over the problems of the nation. Madison

Dolley Madison was noted for her parties, her gowns, and her gracious manners.

continued to remodel his home, rebuilding foundations and chimneys and installing an ice house (one of the first in Virginia) to keep cool drinks and ice cream available for his many visitors.

England was not listening to Madison's messages, still insisting on the United States closing its trade with France. However, it did offer to pay for the 1807 attack on the frigate *Chesapeake*. (After refusing to allow the British to search the warship for possible deserters, the Americans were fired upon and three sailors were killed.) By this time, the United States' Nonintercourse Act was beginning to hurt the British people who depended on America for much of their food. Madison's steady and consistent answer to all British offers was that the ban on trade would be lifted only if the Orders in Council was cancelled and the harassment of American ships stopped. He threatened war. The British scoffed at that. "We will have no war," they said.[4]

All of the messages, threats, and demands that had to travel back and forth across the Atlantic took weeks, even months, to reach the other side. The time lost was critical. Governments could topple, kings could die, Parliament could change in the time it took for communications to arrive.

At last, Madison, who had tried almost everything possible to stop British arrogance and disrespect for American rights, started preparing for the war he wanted to avoid. He waited in vain for the United States warship *Hornet* to bring a reply to his last request to

England to nullify the Orders in Council. He told Congress that war had to be risked, and he asked for money for defense—to build more ships and to reorganize the militia forces. He signed the official declaration of war on June 18, 1812.

All during his failed attempts to bring an end to the hostilities, Madison declared he believed England's true purpose was "to throttle—by keeping American [trade] from growing commercially—a potential rival."[5] As a result of England's actions, he said, American trade on the high seas was being crippled. As a nation, the United States refused to be abused any more. Only war would settle the differences between the two countries. He told Congress that "peace as we now have it is disgraceful, and war honorable."[6] If Madison had tried any other course after all attempts at reconciliation had failed, "he would have been a discredited President, and might have been impeached," one of his biographers wrote.[7]

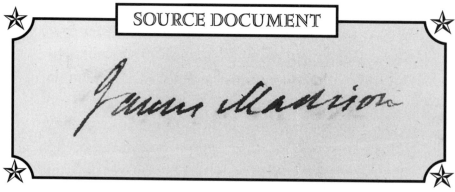

SOURCE DOCUMENT

Shown here is Madison's famous signature to a document issued in his presidential years.

It was not until August that a reply came to Madison's last appeal. The United States learned that Britain had finally yielded and repealed the Orders in Council. That happened just one day before the United States declared war.

It seemed that England had at last decided it had enough of American opposition and wanted to concentrate on the struggle with France. The loss of American markets was affecting the British people. There were demands from Parliament to stop hostilities.

However, it was too late to stop the war. The question was, Could it really have been avoided? Hindsight says "No." War could not have been avoided. England's other offenses would have threatened United States sovereignty if war in 1812 had not settled them once and for all. The British in Canada had been aiding the Native Americans under Tecumseh, encouraging them to resist American advances on their land. If war was to come with England later over the control of the northwestern frontier, the American westerners were ready. They even wanted to take possession of Canada and force the British from the North American continent. In Congress, the fiery Henry Clay declared, "I am not for stopping at Quebec. I would take the whole continent."[8]

In Florida, American settlers would also welcome war against England. Spain, which claimed control of all Florida, was allied with England. Without the backing of England, Florida could easily become a United States territory. By encouraging settlers to move to

Florida, Madison had "enlarged the scope of American national interest and made clear the danger of European inroads on the western hemisphere."[9]

As the war continued, not very successfully at first from the American viewpoint, the Federalists kept up criticism of the President for everything that went wrong. They called the conflict "Mr. Madison's War."

As an executive, James Madison certainly had made mistakes. His first cabinet appointments were not brilliant. Robert Smith, his first secretary of state, was a blunderer who ridiculed Madison as timid and fearful. When Madison discovered Smith was also disloyal, he dismissed him and appointed James Monroe in Smith's place. Always considered a friend, although at times in opposition to Madison, Monroe proved to be efficient and loyal. The other cabinet members were, as Henry Adams said, "the least satisfactory . . . any President had known."[10]

When his first term neared an end, Madison's re-election was contested by DeWitt Clinton of New York, whom the Federalists supported. The opposition to Madison was strong, reflecting the view of some citizens that "our rulers can neither make war nor conclude peace."[11]

James Madison's election for a second term was far from certain.

9

PRESIDENT—
SECOND TERM

President Madison was reelected in November 1812, although by a narrower margin than in 1808. He gave his inaugural speech in a "lackluster" way.[1] Not many people were convinced when he said he had hope of United States victory due to the "inherent strength of the people . . . their virtue and values."[2]

There were many problems facing Madison as the war went on. The Army was poorly trained, and many of the generals were incompetent. Defeats of American forces on the frontier at Detroit and Fort Erie were disasters due to a lack of warships on the Great Lakes to support land attacks. Although Congress voted to build ten new ships, that was a mere token compared to the seven hundred British warships. The United States could not break the British blockade of the American coast, nor drive out patrolling enemy warships.

The Federalists opposed Congress's attempt to raise taxes to support the war effort. The government had to borrow millions of dollars from private financiers. Some of the New England Federalists withheld their militias and looked the other way while American shippers smuggled goods to the enemy. There was even talk of New England seceding from the Union. The President was accused of being tricked into war.

In the summer of 1813, Madison was stricken with a fever and lay seriously ill. When he recovered, he replaced some generals. Then the Navy showed what it could do if properly equipped. The frigate *United States* demolished the British *Macedonia* on the high seas.

Congress agreed to build more ships, encouraged by the success of Oliver Hazard Perry in regaining control of Lake Erie. The battles of Lake Champlain and Fort Niagara were American victories. On the frontier, the tide began to turn. Generals William Henry Harrison and Winfield Scott won battles against the British and their Native American allies in the Michigan territory. Madison decided to send troops to Florida to ward off the British threat to occupy that area.

In 1813, Czar Alexander of Russia offered to mediate to end the war. His offer was accepted by Madison, as the czar was held in great respect in Europe. Albert Gallatin was sent to join John Quincy Adams, the American minister to Russia. At Madison's request, Payne Todd, twenty-one years old, went along as secretary to Gallatin. Madison hoped that association with Gallatin and his son, who accompanied his father and was near Payne's age, would exert a good influence on Payne. The young man was rapidly becoming the playboy of Washington, with no interest in going to college or preparing for a profession.

The peace commission members met in Ghent, a city in Belgium. Madison sent two more representatives to join Gallatin—Henry Clay and Jonathan Russell. Nothing was heard from the peace commission for many months. When news came, it was not encouraging.

Then came the worst—the British attack on the United States capital. Fifty British warships had anchored in Chesapeake Bay, only two days' march to Washington, D.C. President Madison had recently returned to the city from Montpelier. He learned that his secretary of war, John Armstrong, had been taking over duties belonging to the President and trying to reorganize the Army. Because there was a report that the British were planning to land, Madison felt that there was a real threat to Baltimore and Washington, D.C. This was not the time to disrupt the defense of the area by dismissing Armstrong. He instructed the secretary of war to see to the security of the region, especially Washington, which he believed would be targeted by the British because it was the seat of the government.[3] Armstrong argued that the object of the British was

Baltimore, not Washington. He failed to carry out the orders Madison, aided by Monroe, gave him.

On August 17, 1814, it was learned that there were four thousand British troops anchored in ships at the Patuxent River, only thirty-five miles from Washington. They started to advance. Madison tried to issue orders to a disorganized American force that had as yet done nothing to stop the British march on the capital. He wanted American soldiers to meet the invaders or to do battle with them along the way. On horseback for the next two days, the President visited the American camp, where he encouraged the soldiers to defend the city. Before he left home, he had warned his wife of possible danger, and she assured him she would save his valuable papers if she had to flee. After hearing more bad news the next day, Madison sent a note by messenger to Mrs. Madison to have her carriage ready at a moment's notice in order to leave Washington. He mentioned a meeting place in Virginia where he would join her.

The whole episode seems like a comedy of errors—except for the tragic aftermath. The British marched into Washington, only minutes after Mrs. Madison had escaped with her husband's papers, the silverware, some treasured books, and a portrait of George Washington hastily removed from its frame and carted away for safekeeping.

The American troops on the field as the British marched into Washington were "undisciplined, ill-armed and positioned so badly that the British defeated them easily."[4] A small defending force at the Capitol was overpowered. At the deserted President's House, British officers immediately devoured the supper which Dolley Madison had laid out, hoping for the safe return of her husband and his party. Then the invading troops torched the house and its elegant furnishings and went on to destroy many government buildings, including the Capitol. They were directed by Admiral Cockburn who sneeringly referred to President Madison as "Jemmy." He was reported to have said, "You may thank old Madison for this destruction; it is he who got you into this scrape. We want to catch him and carry him to England."[5]

Luckily, a storm of hurricane force chased the British back to their ships and quenched the fires in the ruined city. As news was learned of the British leaving, the Madisons returned to Washington. Amid the

The Capitol was destroyed by British soldiers in the War of 1812.

The President's House was also destroyed by a fire set by the British.

devastation, a group of citizens met Madison and told him they wanted to send notice to the British commander that they were ready to surrender. The President forbade it, saying he was determined to resist.

President and Mrs. Madison then went to the home of Dolley's sister Anna. Only a few private homes had been destroyed by the British. Later they moved into the Octagon House, loaned to them by the French ambassador. They never lived in the White House (as it was called after its restoration) again, because it was not ready for occupancy until 1817, after Madison had left office.

Madison was soundly criticized for the destruction of Washington, D.C., but most citizens placed blame on the secretary of war, John Armstrong. Even the militia denounced him. He was fired and James Monroe took on the additional duties of secretary of war. In September, only a month after the burning of Washington, the President addressed Congress in the Post Office building, one of the few public buildings spared. He mentioned recent victories over the enemy. Under competent generals, the Americans had turned back a British march on Baltimore, and had driven out Admiral Cockburn and his forces. Then the Americans withstood a British bombardment on Baltimore's nearby Fort McHenry. Francis Scott Key, acting as a messenger from Madison to arrange a prisoner of war exchange, was held overnight on one of the British ships in the harbor. He watched the battle and "by the dawn's early light," saw the American flag still flying over the fort. Later, inspired by the experience, he wrote "The Star-Spangled Banner."

Soon after, news came that a British army moving toward Albany, New York, from Montreal in Canada, had been driven back by the Americans. Some considered that event to be the turning point in the war.

Madison waited for word from the American peace commissioners under Gallatin, now in London for many months. Dolley Madison was waiting for a letter from Payne. The London newspapers continued their taunts against Madison and the United States. "No treaty can be made," one declared, "our demands [are] Submission!"[6] When word finally came from London, it was seen that the British were asking the United States to give up most of Maine and the Newfoundland fishing rights, to make the Northwest Territory a buffer Native American state, and to yield use of the Mississippi River. The absurdity of these demands was recognized and they were quickly rejected by Madison.[7]

The majority of Federalists in Congress decided to oppose President Madison's policies in the fall 1814 congressional elections. They were triumphant, and Madison was described as looking "miserably shattered and woe-begone."[8]

Now the newspapers in England encouraged the eastern states, especially New England, to separate from the "mad Virginians," and to "renew their connections with England."[9] There were calls at home for Madison to resign. Prospects for peace were dark. In one of her letters, Dolley Madison wrote that her husband had not been well since they moved to Octagon House, and their servants were constantly sick from living in a damp cellar.[10]

War on the southern frontier under Andrew Jackson seemed to promise a more hopeful result. He had conquered the Native Americans and won control of most of Alabama. He was thus able to prevent British attempts to install themselves along the Gulf Coast.

There were reports of a possible British attack on New Orleans, Louisana. Madison and Monroe ordered more men and supplies for Jackson. By the end of 1814, the British army was ashore near New Orleans and Jackson began to fortify the city and prepare for battle.

The government was soon to "pass from gloom to glory."[11]

Although the great Battle of New Orleans took place on January 8, 1815, the rest of the country did not hear of it until a month later. Jackson had stationed his forces behind a fortified barracks with a swamp between them and the oncoming British soldiers. The latter had no choice but a frontal attack, and were mowed down. Their bravery in marching into the assault was cited by both sides. Over two thousand British troops were killed, wounded, or captured. Only thirteen Americans were killed and sixty wounded. Jackson's "rag tag" army finished the war.[12]

Ten days after the news of Jackson's victory, a dispatch from Ghent arrived. A peace treaty had been signed several days before the Battle of New Orleans. There were wild celebrations in the streets all over America. The greatest victory since Yorktown and the signing of a peace treaty inspired a national pride that wiped out all the humiliations of the war.

Things had changed for the better in England also. The Duke of Wellington, the great war hero of the Napoleonic Wars, had declared that conquest of the United States was impossible. Great Britain could not afford to continue such a war. The British cabinet agreed. The Prince Regent, eldest son of King George III, replacing his ailing father, signed the treaty to end hostilities.

By standing up to Britain, the United States had won

a second war for independence. The former colonies were now on the way to becoming a world power. The Treaty of Ghent restored the status quo, cancelling the tough terms England had demanded and returning all the American territory occupied by the British forces. Also, rights to the Mississippi River, the Great Lakes, and the Newfoundland fishing banks were recognized as American possessions. The grievances against impressment of American sailors and hijacking of American ships were not mentioned, but such practices were understood to be over.

Trade everywhere was opened again, manufacturing increased, and housing boomed. World respect for the American nation was not only increased, it was never again questioned.

A new age of growth and prosperity seemed just ahead. Now, in the "era of good feelings," "Mr. Madison's peace" was praised. Although he had been engaged in a war which, with all its mistakes, could have brought Madison down, it finally accomplished vital, far-reaching effects for his country.[13]

The President was inspired with new life and vigor. Dolley Madison lit candles that glowed from every window of Octagon House. Soon she would be entertaining again in a larger residence known as the Seven Buildings.

That summer, the Madisons returned to Montpelier. Madison had to repair the long neglect of his fields and struggle for economic recovery. This was all the more important because of bad news from Gallatin about Payne Todd. While abroad, the young man had exhausted the funds given him by his stepfather for his expenses and had run up large gambling debts, which Gallatin had paid. Madison settled that and would be doing more of the same in the years ahead.

In Madison's last year in office, Dolley Madison outdid herself in entertaining. Never had Washington seen such a glittering season. Nor had Mrs. Madison ever looked as queenly, in her costly gowns and headdresses. She was called the idol of Washington. At the Madisons' New Year's reception at the Seven Buildings, Dolley was wearing a tiara encrusted with sapphires, Madison's latest gift to her.

During his final months, the President endorsed the

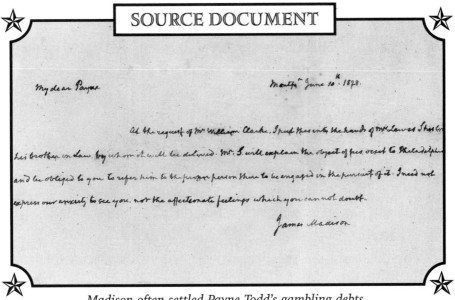

Madison often settled Payne Todd's gambling debts.

renewal of the national bank which he had opposed when Alexander Hamilton was in favor of it. Now he felt that it was necessary to uphold public credit and to have a stable financial institution for government securities. He also recommended a tariff to protect domestic products and wanted to establish a national university in Washington, D.C. The latter request was rejected, but his proposal to grant pensions to disabled war veterans was supported.

Madison told his party advisors he would not run again, thus making permanent (for many years) the precedent of two terms only, set by Washington and Jefferson. Madison supported James Monroe as his successor and saw him elected to the presidency in 1816. The greatly weakened Federalists deplored the fact that a fourth Virginian was to lead the nation.[14] The rest of the country, however, still praising Madison, felt no such dismay. Even John Adams, the Federalist ex-President, expressed an admiring opinion of the departing President. He said that Madison's administration, "notwithstanding a thousand faults and blunders, has acquired more glory, and established more union than all his three predecessors."[15] Madison himself was satisfied that the American people had reached forty years in safety and success, as an independent nation under the Constitution he had helped to create. Already, he was being called the father of the Constitution.

After Monroe's inauguration, the Madisons stayed in

SOURCE DOCUMENT

James Madison's enduring legacy to America was the Constitution.

Washington for several weeks. There were many parties and celebrations in their honor. The Monroes moved into the newly restored President's House, now to be called the White House. On January 1, 1818, it was open to the public for the traditional New Year's reception.

In the spring of 1817, the Madisons left Washington for their final return to Montpelier. This time, they started off on one of the new steamboats that went several miles down the Potomac River to a landing where their carriage awaited them. They finished the trip on land and arrived in Montpelier two days sooner than formerly. Steam was just beginning to change the means of transportation in the country. Railroads would be the next big improvement in travel.

The newly restored President's House, now called the White House, was opened to the public on January 1, 1818.

People who were on the steamboat with the Madisons that day in 1817 remarked on the ex-President's high spirits. He was unusually talkative and cheerful, "Like a schoolboy on a long vacation," they said.[16]

Retirement was a pleasant prospect.

10

ACTIVE RETIREMENT

H ome at last, the Madisons settled down contentedly to live in the place Madison loved best. He could enjoy visits from relatives and friends. Above all, he was only a day's ride away from Thomas Jefferson.

The Montpelier mansion, with its spacious rooms, book-lined walls, and works of art, was designed for comfort and hospitality. Madison's mother still lived in her own quarters in the south wing, where she spent her time reading and knitting. Her many grandchildren came often to see her, and Dolley Madison's several nieces and nephews came too. James and Dolley were uncle and aunt to all—his and hers alike. As always, Dolley's sister Anna, her closest and dearest relative, and her children were often there. There was never a pause in the steady stream of visitors to Montpelier. They were all welcomed and treated with true southern hospitality. Dolley Madison never knew beforehand how many people to expect for dinner or how many beds would be occupied, but she never lost her welcoming smiles and attention to her guests' comfort. Dinner usually took two hours. Afterward the company moved to the drawing room to hear Madison's stimulating conversation and his stories about his long service in government affairs. It was like "living history" to hear him, as one visitor said.[1]

Dolley Madison was the household manager. Her husband managed the plantation, riding around daily on his horse Liberty to check on crops and animals (there were sheep and cows as well as horses). The slave quarters, called Walnut Grove, were at some distance from the Madisons' house.

The view outside never failed to charm visitors as well as the Madisons themselves. The Blue Ridge Mountains provided splendid scenery, with shifting light and shade. Nearer, there were flower and vegetable gardens, towering trees that shaded the house, fields of tobacco and wheat, and then the forest meeting the mountains. All of it provided, so it was said, "a delightful refreshment to the eye."[2]

Madison and Jefferson had always been interested in agriculture and the science of growing food and enriching the soil. Jefferson called his friend "the best farmer in the world."[3] In 1818, Madison was elected president of his county agricultural society. He spoke and wrote about crop rotation, scientifically breeding livestock, reforestation, keeping the balance of nature, and many ways to protect the living environment. His writings received worldwide attention.

Madison's closer presence meant many visits and long conversations with Jefferson. They wrote letters when the weather kept them apart. Jefferson wanted Madison's help in establishing his dream—a university for Virginia. The College of William and Mary was for the elite, the wealthy. The University of Virginia would be for the people—and the people's children. After Jefferson succeeded in getting the state legislature to provide funding, a site was chosen in Charlottesville. Jefferson could view it from Monticello through his telescope.

Madison joined his friend in this worthy project. He firmly believed in improving higher education in the republic. While President, he had succeeded in enlarging the United States Military Academy at West Point. He had said, in a message to Congress, that without education "the blessings of liberty can not be fully enjoyed or long preserved."[4]

Jefferson delayed the first meeting of the new university's executive board until Madison could join the group. When the board met in 1819, Madison helped to elect Jefferson the university's first rector, as the board's leader was called. Funds were limited, but to offset that, the board had a great asset in the "architectural genius" of the rector, who donated his services.[5] Jefferson drafted the plans and constantly visited the site as the buildings were being constructed. He also planned the curriculum and hired the professors.

Madison served faithfully on the board of directors for eleven years. Toward the end of Jefferson's life, the two old friends proudly accompanied the Marquis de Lafayette on a tour of their university. The French hero of the American Revolution was visiting the United States in 1824. The following year, Jefferson and Madison were dismayed by a student riot on the campus. Jefferson tried to talk to the demonstrators but without any effect, and Madison saw the tears in his friend's eyes. The rioting students were protesting the university's decision to hire foreign professors.

Before he died, Jefferson asked Madison to carry on his work at the university. Madison did that after Jefferson's death on July 4, 1826, and served as rector for several years.

The nation wrestled with two big problems during the years of Madison's retirement. Slavery was one. Although he was against it, he could see no way of getting rid of it. He was "a southerner long embarrassed by the fact of slavery, but also the son of a planter who owned 100 field hands."[6] He knew slavery was a curse, "the original sin of the African trade," but he also knew it was impossible to destroy without danger of war or secession.[7] Back in 1785, Madison had spoken in the

Virginia Assembly in favor of a bill Jefferson had introduced that would gradually abolish slavery in Virginia. The bill was quickly and overwhelmingly rejected.[8]

Madison had often discussed the slavery question with Jefferson, who experienced the same frustration, as well as with other eminent men like Henry Clay and John Marshall who also felt as he did. One proposal made by those who wanted to eliminate slavery was for the government to set aside land in the West as a refuge for the African Americans who would be freed. This meant that the government would have to pay slave owners to free their slaves. Slaves were a financial asset for the southern planters whose fortunes rose and fell from other things they could not control like crop failures and weather disasters. The resettlement of African Americans in the West never came to pass. In addition to the enormous amount of money involved, the West rapidly became occupied by white settlers who found land prices cheaper there than in the eastern part of the country.

Another attempt to lessen the "curse" of slavery was the work of the American Colonization Society, founded in 1820, to resettle freed slaves in Africa. In 1822, James Madison accepted the presidency of the society. The organization encouraged owners to free slaves who could then go to Liberia, a colony established on the west coast of Africa. By 1830, less than three thousand American freed slaves accepted the offer, while sixty thousand were added to the slave population annually. Of his own slaves, Madison said that none were willing to settle in Liberia.

Madison could only hope that as time went on slavery would be gradually eliminated. He believed that even a slow and uncertain progress toward abolition was preferable to the continuance of slavery. In 1829, when writing to Lafayette, who had asked if a policy of emancipation of slaves was ever considered, Madison said that it "would have been a spark to a mass of Gunpowder."[9]

The slavery problem—then—seemed impossible to

SOURCE DOCUMENT

Madison became president of the American Colonization Society in 1822. This is his certificate of membership.

resolve. However, in the 1820s and 1830s, when some southerners spoke of secession if the North tried to change the status of slaves, Madison's chief concern was nullification—and its partner, secession. Nullification was the belief that a state might reject any federal law it considered unconstitutional. According to one of Madison's biographers, nullification was "the greatest trial of his retirement."[10]

In 1828, South Carolina, led by John C. Calhoun, pushed to nullify a high tariff imposed by the federal government. The old cry of states' rights was raised again, as were claims that any state had the right to nullify or make void any federal law it considered harmful. Of course Madison spoke out against this, and wrote articles for the newspapers. He was accused of denying his former positions. It was pointed out that he had upheld states' rights in 1798 and now spoke for an indivisible Union. He opposed a national bank in 1787 but later, as President, agreed to the bank's recharter. Were there two James Madisons?

Madison admitted it was true he had always been in favor of states' rights, but never to the point of dissolving the Union. The Constitution was a pact to which all the states were parties. "What madness in the South," he said, "to look for greater safety in disunion . . . worse than jumping from the Frying pan into the fire."[11]

When it looked as if South Carolina was going to carry out its threat to secede, President Andrew Jackson ordered the Army to Charleston. Violence seemed near.

Then, in time to prevent bloodshed, Senator Henry Clay arranged a compromise in the United States Senate. The compromise lowered the tariff and turned aside the immediate danger. But Madison remained uneasy about the future.[12] He believed reason and restraint were necessary in a republican form of government if it was to survive. Over all, he was hopeful the Union would survive even though the nation's population was increasing rapidly. It had tripled in one generation, going from 4 million in 1790 to 12 million in 1830. After all, it was he who had claimed in the Constitutional Convention that, when the nation expanded, government by the people would work as well if not better than in a smaller population.

In 1829, new problems in Virginia prompted the call for a Constitutional Convention to revise the old State Constitution that Madison had witnessed in 1776. His neighbors in Orange County elected him as a delegate. At age seventy-eight, he agreed to go to Richmond for the Convention. He and his wife stayed in Richmond for three months, at the home of one of Dolley's cousins.

The Convention was a collection of notables—James Monroe, now also an ex-President, future President John Tyler, Chief Justice John Marshall, and Madison's old-time opponent, John Randolph. People at the convention had great respect for Madison, who was elected to the important Committee on Proportional Representation. His small but erect figure in his customary black style of dress, now old-fashioned, was a reminder of past history. To the younger delegates, who knew him only by reputation, he was like a mythical character coming to life. When he spoke, his voice was low, but clearly heard in the hushed assembly.

Madison favored giving voting rights to all men who paid taxes, not just to landowners as was the current practice then. Householders, heads of families, should be allowed to vote, he said. That met with majority approval but the next part of Madison's proposal did not. Up to this time the voters in eastern Virginia, many of whom were plantation owners and slaveholders, could add all of their slaves to the population count. This practice gave them more representation in Virginia's House of Delegates than non-slaveholders had. The westerners, who were settling in the

Madison spoke at the Virginia Constitutional Convention of 1829–1830.

developing part of the state, opposed the slave count. Madison suggested a compromise that would allow the easterners to count just three fifths of their slaves, not all of them. This would reduce the slave owners' representation. Madison's compromise did not pass.

His last public appearance was over. The Madisons went home to Montpelier. He settled down to a large task, one he worked on constantly during his last years: arranging his papers. Over the course of many years, he had collected a huge amount of writings, notes, and correspondence. His secretary, Edward Coles, helped, retrieving many letters Madison had sent to friends and associates. When Coles left after a few years, Dolley Madison helped to transcribe the notes and reports.

Madison knew his papers relating to the Constitution were valuable—primary sources about the Constitution—and his greatest asset. He told his wife she was to sell them, preferably to the government, after he was gone. He judged they would be worth enough money to take care of her in comfort for the rest of her life.

Like many planters in the South, Jefferson included, Madison was rich only in land—which he had to mortgage sometimes to raise money—and slaves, whom he had to support. He was a humane owner and rarely sold a slave. Another big expense Madison had was Payne Todd. His stepson accumulated so many debts that he was threatened with debtors' prison. Madison always paid Payne's bills and kept the bad news from

Dolley Madison as long as he could. When Payne had exhausted all the ways he could raise money, he returned to Montpelier and lived there during Madison's last years. Madison knew that, through Dolley, Payne would probably inherit Montpelier, but that was something beyond his control.

He had made his will. Dolley would inherit the land, the house, and the slaves. She could sell all of her inheritance if she wished. Whatever money he had was to be divided among his nieces and nephews, or their children. Madison also directed that Dolley Madison could keep three hundred volumes of his valuable library and give the rest to the University of Virginia. After Jefferson's death, Madison himself had arranged to have his friend's extensive book collection given to the Library of Congress.

As Madison's health declined in his last years, he had to be carried from bed to couch or chair by his faithful slave, Paul Jennings. His mind was still bright and alert, and he enjoyed visitors who came and talked with him. His wife and his niece, Nelly Willis, were his constant attendants.

The story is told that in late June 1836, it was obvious that Madison was sinking fast and could not live many more days. It was suggested by friends, or in some versions of the story, his doctor, that he take some medication to prolong his life until July 4. That would be the sixtieth anniversary of the Declaration of Independence. Also, July 4, by strange coincidence, was the day three former Presidents died—Jefferson and Adams on the same day, July 4, 1826, and Monroe on July 4, 1831. However, Madison rejected the suggestion, saying that a man died in his own time. His final day was June 28, 1836. He was eighty-five.

In a note he left, which was opened by relatives, he gave his last advice to his country. "The thought nearest

James Madison died on June 28, 1836.

to my heart and deepest in my convictions is that the Union of the States be cherished and perpetuated."[13]

James Madison's body was buried in the Montpelier family plot half a mile from his house. There were eulogies and memorial services all over the country. It was noted that Madison was the last of the nation builders, who spoke the words "of peace—of harmony—of union."[14]

Dolley Madison stayed at Montpelier until the fall of 1837, when she returned to Washington, D.C. She had many friends and relatives there. Her young niece, Anna Payne, had come to live with her as companion and secretary. Dolley and Anna settled in a small house on Lafayette Square, across the street from the White House. It was a small but now valuable legacy in Madison's will.

After the bequests to nieces and nephews were settled, and the debts and mortgages on Montpelier land paid off, Dolley had few financial resources. The upkeep of Montpelier forced her to sell it after a few years and she used most of the money to help her son Payne, as usual. His latest unsuccessful project was a get-rich-quick scheme raising silkworms. Dolley Madison would eventually try to sell off her furniture, paintings, silver plate, books, and mementos, until friends intervened to help her. Daniel Webster was in Congress then; although not a member of Madison's party, he helped Dolley Madison in several ways. One way was his purchase of Paul Jennings, James

I consider my Husband's writings sacred, and no more to be infringed or altered than his last Will. He desired me to read them over and if any letter, line or word struck me as being calculated to injure the feelings of any one, or wrong in them that I would withdraw them, or if he was satisfied that one name had been used in mistake for another which he wished might give place to the right one. The slight corrections therefore are consonant to his wishes and directions, and made with my concurrence.

D. P. Madison

16. March 1839

This is a letter to Congress in which Dolley Madison explains her husband's wishes about his letters.

Madison's slave, whom Webster then set free. In later life, Jennings wrote a book about his life with Madison.

The big task Dolley Madison faced in Washington was to arrange the purchase of James Madison's papers, over which he had worked so long. She offered them to the government. Congress dallied for four years over the purchase, then agreed to pay $25,000, a much smaller sum than Madison expected. The papers were turned over to the Library of Congress, and Dolley was satisfied, knowing that her husband's papers would be safe for future generations.

Dolley Madison's return to the social round of Washington affairs was welcomed. All the Presidents during her time treated her with honor and respect. When she entertained in her small house on the two big holidays of the year, January 1 and July 4, people crowded in to see her. She enjoyed parties, matchmaking, and visitors. The words describing her were, as before, "elegant," "charming," "gracious." When she died, on July 12, 1849, it was said that "she had become a legend before her death."[15]

11

THE MADISON LEGACY

J ames Madison is best remembered for his work in framing and writing the Constitution of the United States. It is right to call him the nation's founder, although he said that was credit he did not deserve, "because the Constitution was the work of many heads and many hands."[1]

President John F. Kennedy said that "Madison was our most under-rated president."[2] In recent years, however, Madison has come into his own. After the bicentennial year of the Constitution in 1987, many books and articles were devoted to Madison's life and achievements. The survival of the Constitution for over two centuries is proof of his faith in the constitutional basis of the American republic. Madison's Constitution has lasted and served very well, withstanding some hard tests over the years.

James Madison was a scholar and an intellectual, probably the best-educated President we have ever had. He never stopped learning. He collected books of the great writers and philosophers at a time when it was necessary to obtain them from abroad. He could read many languages—French, Italian, Spanish, Hebrew, and, from his school days, Latin and Greek. He was also a skillful writer, able to simplify and condense difficult concepts so they could be understood by all. His writings take up volumes, and to this day, are studied by scholars of constitutional governments. Reading some of his writings, one is struck by the directness of his language. It seems as modern as today. "If men were angels, no government would be necessary,"[3] he said, and "Government must never be too strong or too weak."[4] Referring to the conflict with Great Britain, he said, "We are teaching the world the great truth that governments do better without kings and nobles than with them."[5]

Madison's career in the service of his country spanned sixty years. He began in 1776 as a young member of the Virginia House of Delegates. There he, like others of like mind, pushed for a new Constitution for Virginia. That in turn inspired the Continental Congress to declare the American colonies' independence from Great Britain on July 4, 1776. From Virginia's legislature, Madison went on to the United States Congress, then to President Jefferson's cabinet, and finally to the presidency itself. "In all of [Madison's] positions, whether elective or appointive, [he] was an intellectual leader, sometimes the leader."[6] By good fortune, his troubled eight years as President ended on a jubilant note when the United States won the War of 1812. He retired with the good will of the nation.

Even after retirement, Madison participated in public affairs by writing and speaking about the issues of his time. He also served as a director of the University of Virginia, founded through his and Jefferson's dedication to the education of the people. One of his biographers said, "No mind has stamped more of its impressions on American institutions than Madison."[7]

Chronology

1751—James Madison was born, first child of James Madison, Sr., and Nelly Conway Madison of Orange County, Virginia, on March 16.

1761—Moved with his family to new home, known as Montpelier.

1762–1767—Attended a plantation boarding school, taught by Donald Robertson.

1767–1769—Tutored at home by the Reverend Thomas Martin in preparation for college.

1769–1772—Studied at the College of New Jersey (Princeton University).

1774—Appointed to Orange County's Committee of Safety.

1775–1783—American armed conflict with Great Britain.

1775—Madison prevented from joining the military because of poor health.

1776—Chosen as delegate to Williamsburg Convention to draft new constitution for Virginia in May; served one term in Virginia's House of Delegates; Declaration of Independence issued by Continental Congress on July 4.

1777—Appointed to Virginia Council of State; friendship with Thomas Jefferson began.

1779—Elected to the Continental Congress in Philadelphia.

1780–1783—Served in Continental Congress.

1783—Engagement to Kitty Floyd made and soon broken; Madison's term in Congress ended.

1784–1787—Elected to Virginia's House of Delegates; served three years.

1787–1788—Elected a delegate to Constitutional Convention; wrote *The Federalist Papers* with Alexander Hamilton and John Jay.

1789–1796—Elected a Congressman from Virginia to the first federal House of Representatives; served eight years.

1794—Married Dolley Payne Todd.

1796—Left Congress; returned to Montpelier.

1800—Appointed secretary of state by President-elect Thomas Jefferson.

1801–1809—Served as secretary of state.

1808—Elected President of the United States.

1809–1817—Served two terms as President.

1812—Declared war on Great Britain in the War of 1812.

1815–1816—Victory at New Orleans ended war; peace treaty signed; was praised for "Mr. Madison's peace."

1817—Returned to Montpelier for remainder of life; worked on getting his papers in order for future publication.

1829—Made last public appearance before the Virginia Convention to revise state Constitution.

1836—Died at Montpelier on June 28, at eighty-five years of age.

Chapter Notes

Chapter 1

1. Jean Fritz, *The Great Little Madison* (New York: G. P. Putnam's Sons, 1989), p. 45.
2. Virginia Moore, *The Madisons: A Biography* (New York: McGraw-Hill, 1979), p. 222.
3. Ibid., p. 221.
4. Ibid., p. 224.

Chapter 2

1. Ralph Ketchum, *James Madison: A Biography* (New York: The Macmillan Co., 1971), p. 17.
2. Virginia Moore, *The Madisons: A Biography* (New York: McGraw-Hill, 1979), p. 25.

Chapter 3

1. Irving Brant, *James Madison: The Virginia Revolutionist, 1751–1780* (Indianapolis: The Bobbs-Merrill Co., 1944), p. 72.
2. Virginia Moore, *The Madisons: A Biography* (New York: McGraw-Hill, 1979), pp. 38–39.
3. Ibid.
4. Ibid., p. 34.

Chapter 4

1. Ralph Ketchum, *James Madison: A Biography* (New York: The Macmillan Co., 1971), p. 81.
2. Robert Allen Rutland, *James Madison: The Founding Father* (New York: Macmillan Publishing Co., 1987), p. 11.

3. Ketchum, p. 73.

4. Ibid., p. 77.

5. Harold S. Schultz, *James Madison* (New York: Twain Publishers, 1970), p. 29.

Chapter 5

1. Harold S. Schultz, *James Madison* (New York: Twain Publishers, 1970), p. 55.

2. Richard B. Morris, *Witnesses at the Creation* (New York: Holt, Rinehart and Winston, 1985), p. 195.

3. Schultz, p. 55.

4. Morris, p. 216.

5. Ibid.

6. Jean Fritz, *The Great Little Madison* (New York: G. P. Putnam's Sons, 1989), p. 45.

7. John D. Hicks, *The Federal Union* (Boston: Houghton Mifflin Co., 1937), pp. 207–208.

8. Robert Allen Rutland, *James Madison: The Founding Father* (New York: Macmillan Publishing Company, 1987), p. 51.

9. Ibid., p. 56.

10. Fritz, p. 56.

11. Willard Sterne Randall, "Thomas Jefferson Takes a Vacation," *American Heritage*, July–August 1996, p. 77.

Chapter 6

1. Ralph Ketchum, *James Madison: A Biography* (New York: The Macmillan Publishing Company, 1971), p. 378.

2. Ibid., p. 382.

3. Ibid., p. 354.

4. Ibid., p. 365.

5. Ibid., p. 388.

Chapter 7

1. John D. Hicks, *The Federal Union* (Boston: Houghton Mifflin Co., 1937), p. 255.

2. Ralph Ketchum, *James Madison: A Biography* (New York: The Macmillan Company, 1971), p. 408.

3. Ibid.

4. Jean Fritz, *The Great Little Madison* (New York: G. P. Putnam's Sons, 1989), p. 87.

5. Ketchum, p. 409.

6. Ibid., p. 420.

7. Ibid., p. 436.

8. Virginia Moore, *The Madisons: A Biography* (New York: McGraw-Hill, 1979), p. 212.

9. Ketchum, p. 436.

10. Moore, p. 201.

Chapter 8

1. Ralph Ketchum, *James Madison: A Biography* (New York: The Macmillan Company, 1971), p. 473.

2. Ibid., p. 467.

3. Ibid., p. 466.

4. Virginia Moore, *The Madisons: A Biography* (New York: McGraw-Hill, 1979), p. 232.

5. Ibid., p. 230.

6. Robert Allen Rutland, *James Madison: The Founding Father* (New York: Macmillan Publishing Co., 1987), p. 226.

7. Ibid., p. 223.

8. John D. Hicks, *The Federal Union* (Boston: Houghton Mifflin Co., 1937), p. 301.

9. Ketchum, p. 502.

10. Rutland, p. 207.

11. Ketchum, p. 588.

Chapter 9

1. Ralph Ketchum, *James Madison: A Biography* (New York: The Macmillan Co., 1971), p. 556.

2. Ibid.

3. Ibid., p. 574.

4. Ibid., p. 578.

5. Ibid., p. 579.

6. Ibid., p. 590.

7. Ibid., p. 591.

8. Ibid., p. 592.

9. Virginia Moore, *The Madisons: A Biography* (New York: McGraw-Hill, 1979), p. 344.

10. Ketchum, p. 594.

11. Moore, p. 344.

12. Robert Allen Rutland, *James Madison: The Founding Father* (New York: Macmillan Publishing Co., 1987), p. 230.

13. Moore, p. 347.

14. Rutland, p. 237.

15. Ibid.

16. Ibid., p. 239.

Chapter 10

1. Drew R. McCoy, *The Last of the Fathers: James Madison and the Republican Legacy* (New York: Cambridge University Press, 1989), p. 1.

2. Harold S. Schultz, *James Madison* (New York: Twain Publishers, 1970), p. 203.

3. Naomi Barry, "Hello Dolley: On the Trail of the Madisons," *Gourmet*, December 1989, p. 234.

4. Robert Allen Rutland, *James Madison: The Founding Father* (New York: Macmillan Publishing Co., 1987), p. 236.

5. Ibid., p. 243.

6. Ibid., p. 239.

7. Ralph Ketchum, *James Madison: A Biography* (New York: The Macmillan Co., 1971), p. 627.

8. Ibid., p. 149.

9. Rutland, p. 247.

10. McCoy, p. 118.

11. Ketchum, p. 646.

12. Jean Fritz, *The Great Little Madison* (New York: G. P. Putnam's Sons, 1989), p. 149.

13. Ketchum, p. 671.

14. Ibid., p. 670.

15. Katharine Anthony, *Dolly Madison: Her Life and Times* (New York: Doubleday and Co., Inc., 1949), p. 406.

Chapter 11

1. Harold S. Schultz, *James Madison* (New York: Twain Publishers, 1970), p. 77.

2. Robert Allen Rutland, *James Madison: The Founding Father* (New York: Macmillan Publishing Co., 1987), p. 252.

3. Saul K. Padover, *The Complete Madison: His Basic Writings* (New York: Harper and Brothers, 1953), p. 13.

4. Ibid., p. 16.

5. Ibid., p. 344.

6. Ibid., p. 4.

7. Drew R. McCoy, *The Last of the Fathers: James Madison and the Republican Legacy* (New York: Cambridge University Press, 1989), p. 17.

Further Reading

Anthony, Katharine. *Dolly Madison: Her Life and Times.* New York: Doubleday and Company, 1949.

Brant, Irving. *James Madison: The Virginia Revolutionist.* Indianapolis: Bobbs-Merrill, 1944.

Clinton, Susan. *James Madison: Encyclopedia of Presidents.* Chicago: Children's Press, 1986.

Friedel, Frank. *The Presidents of the United States of America.* Washington, D.C.: The White House Historical Association, 1982.

Fritz, Jean. *The Great Little Madison.* New York: G. P. Putnam's Sons, 1989.

Ketchum, Ralph. *James Madison: A Biography.* New York: The Macmillan Co., 1971.

Klepthor, Margaret Brown. *The First Ladies.* Washington, D.C.: The White House Historical Association, 1981.

McCoy, Drew R. *The Last of the Fathers: James Madison and the Republican Legacy.* New York: Cambridge University Press, 1989.

Moore, Virginia. *The Madisons: A Biography.* New York: McGraw-Hill, 1979.

Morris, Richard B. *Witnesses at the Creation.* New York: Holt, Rinehart and Winston, 1985.

Padover, Saul K. *The Complete Madison: His Basic Writings.* New York: Harper, 1953.

Rutland, Robert Allen. *James Madison: The Founding Father.* New York: Macmillan Publishing Co., 1987.

Schultz, Harold S. *James Madison.* New York: Twain Publishers, 1970.

Internet Addresses

For further research on James Madison:

Library of Congress

Web Site—http://www.loc.gov.

National Archives

Web Site—http://www.nara.gov.

E-mail—inquire@nara:gov.

University of Virginia

Web Site—http://www.lib.virginia.edu

Harvard University Library

Web Site—http://www.harvard.edu

New York Public Library Research Libraries

Web Site—http://www.nypl.org

Virginia State Library and Archives

Web Site—http://leo.vsla.edu

Index